SERIOUS MONEY

SERIOUS MONEY

FUNDRAISING AND CONTRIBUTING IN PRESIDENTIAL NOMINATION CAMPAIGNS

Clifford W. Brown, Jr.
Union College

Lynda W. Powell
University of Rochester

Clyde Wilcox
Georgetown University

CAMBRIDGE
UNIVERSITY PRESS

3/00

Published by the Press Syndicate of the University of Cambridge
The Pitt Building, Trumpington Street, Cambridge CB2 1RP
40 West 20th Street, New York, NY 10011–4211, USA
10 Stamford Road, Oakleigh, Melbourne 3166, Australia

First published 1995

Printed in the United States of America

Library of Congress Cataloging-in-Publication Data
Brown, Clifford W. (Clifford Waters), 1942–
Serious money : fundraising and contributing in presidential
nomination campaigns / Clifford W. Brown, Jr., Lynda W. Powell,
Clyde Wilcox.
   p. cm.
Includes bibliographical references and index.
ISBN 0–521–44058–0. – ISBN 0–521–49780–9 (pbk.)
1. Campaign funds – United States. 2. Presidents – United States
– Nomination.   I. Powell, Lynda W.   II. Wilcox, Clyde, 1953–
III. Title.
JK 1991.B76   1995
324.7'8'0973–dc20   95–10760
                                                                   CIP

A catalog record for this book is available from the British Library.

ISBN 0–521–44058–0 hardback
ISBN 0–521–49780–9 paperback

To the memory of Marver Bernstein, William Riker, and Charles Tidmarch – colleagues, friends, and mentors. Their passion for the study of politics was unsurpassed.

Contents

Figures and tables

Acknowledgments

We wish to acknowledge the help of many people without whom this book could not have been written. First, we are exceedingly grateful to our respondents from 1972, 1988, and 1992, whose cooperation was essential to this endeavor. We are also grateful for the insights given us by the following experts on campaigns and campaign finance whom we interviewed: Margaret Alexander, Mike Berman, Richard Bond, Anthony Corrado, Roger Craver, Kristin Demong, Irwin Harrison, Celinda Lake, Michael MacLeod, Terry McAuliffe, Scott McKenzie, Hal Malchow, Philip Smith, and Richard Weingold.

We wish to acknowledge the assistance of Herbert Alexander, who helped us obtain the original lists of names of contributors used to draw the sample for the 1972 survey. We also wish to acknowledge the efforts of Roman Hedges, who worked with two of us in conducting that survey. He played a major role in designing the 1972 questionnaire, drawing the sample, carrying out the survey, and analyzing the results. To the extent that the present study builds upon our previous joint research, we are greatly indebted to him. We also wish to thank Robert Biersack, who provided us with many numbers, answered many questions, and helped us obtain from the Federal Election Commission the computerized lists of names of individual contributors to federal candidates in the 1987–88 and 1991–92 election cycles.

G. Bingham Powell, Jr., Lee Sigelman, and Robert Biersack read and commented on the manuscript. We greatly appreciate their many helpful suggestions which have contributed extensively to this book. We also wish to acknowledge the many insightful and supportive comments of three anonymous reviewers of the prospectus and of the manuscript. These, too, were exceedingly helpful. The contributions of all these readers have made a great difference in the quality of the final product. Needless to say the responsibility for the content of this book, and especially any errors contained therein, is our own.

We also wish to thank the following, who helped fund our research: the Union College Faculty Research Fund, chaired by Associate Dean Terry Weiner; the Department of Political Science at the University of Rochester; the Department of Government at Georgetown University; and the Society for the Scientific Study of Religion.

Our chairs, colleagues, and departmental staffs at the University of Rochester, Georgetown University, and Union College have enthusiastically supported and contributed to this project in numerous ways from the start, and we are very appreciative of their backing. We wish to acknowledge the assistance of April Morgan, Eleanor Neff Powell, and Marianne Moore, who assisted either in the collection of the data or in the preparation of the manuscript. We wish to thank, too, our editor, Alex Holzman, our production editor, Katharita Lamoza, and our typographer and indexer, George Madden.

We also wish to thank the members of our respective families and extended families for their patience, understanding, and encouragement during the conduct of the surveys and the writing of this book.

1. Introduction

Robert Farmer, a major fundraiser for both Michael Dukakis and Bill Clinton, offered this blunt assessment of Paul Tsongas's decision to quit the 1992 presidential race: "People don't lose campaigns. They run out of money and can't get their planes in the air. That's the reality" *(Congressional Quarterly Weekly Report,* 1992). Although Tsongas himself may have had several reasons for dropping out, he highlighted finance as one of them: "If you have no resources to fight back with, you are defenseless in this business. . . . Michael Dukakis had the most money and could take out Dick Gephardt and everybody else, and Bill Clinton basically did the same thing" ("MacNeil/Lehrer Newshour" 1992).

There can be little doubt that money is important: in seven of the eight major-party presidential nomination contests that took place since the current financial rules of engagement went into effect in 1980, the eventual winner had the largest amount of cash in the bank on January 1 when the process started in earnest. Caution, of course, is warranted in assuming a causal connection here. Those who have the most cash reserves at the start of the process (or who eventually raise the most money) do so for a reason, and the political resources that enable candidates to win the nomination may also be those resources that enable them to raise large amounts of money and raise them early. Attractive, viable candidates tend to receive more money as well as more votes.

It is also wrong to assume that just because a candidate raises a lot of money he or she will do well. In 1988, Pat Robertson raised more than George Bush, and in 1980 John Connolly's single "twelve million dollar" delegate earned a permanent place in presidential nomination lore. Still, it is difficult to deny the importance of large and early cash reserves in the nomination process: the strong evidence is that they are a necessary, though certainly not sufficient, condition for victory.

The role of money in determining political success is a controversial one, and the relatively small number of candidates competing in any given presidential nomination campaign makes formal estimation of the effects of campaign money very difficult. Furthermore, studies have shown that losers often outspend winners in given contests, including presidential primaries. For example, on Super Tuesday in 1988, Robertson and Dole outspent a victorious Bush in several states, and Gore outspent a victorious Jackson in several others.[1] Bush's winning margin in southern Super Tuesday states was not associated with either his spending or that of his opponents (Norrander 1989). Later in the year, Jackson lost to Dukakis (while outspending him) in Ohio, Pennsylvania, and California.[2] To focus narrowly on whether money is decisive in helping a candidate surmount the hurdle of a given primary, however, is to ignore the larger role of money in a presidential nomination contest, which has many events spread over time, and where the ability to sustain an effort in the long run may be just as important as prevailing in any given single event. Hurdle power is very important, but so is staying power. Money arguably underwrites both.

The advantages of early money

The advantages of money, and especially *early* money, are widely recognized. First, the press uses fiscal solvency as an indicator of a candidate's chances of success (Paolino 1994), publicizes the financial assets of each candidate, and often uses early money to determine who is the "front-runner" before what John Kessel (1980) calls the "Initial Contests" give a clearer indication of who is really ahead. This was certainly the case in 1988 and 1992.

Money raised and spent early can itself enhance perceptions of viability before the real tests occur, and the image of viability, in turn, helps a candidate attract volunteers and additional contributions from those anxious to back a winner. Early money also begets more money through the federal match, and those who raise the most money can almost always expect to receive the most from the initial match, thereby widening the financial gap between themselves and those who raise less.

In addition, money buys access to the media, which enables less-well-known candidates to gain name recognition and deliver a message, especially in the early days of the process. Among relatively unknown candidates, money is essential to establishing an identity (Wilcox 1991). Money may not always be fully effective in overcoming the free media exposure of opposition candidates or in undercutting their support, but it does help relatively unknown candidates gain a wider audience.

In this respect, money is a crucial ingredient in "defining" a candidate for the voters. Candidates who have money can define themselves – and negatively define others as well. Those who lack money will be defined by those who have it. Tsongas put it well on the day he quit the race, even though this was not a comprehensive explanation of his decision to withdraw:

What happened to us in the big states [with expensive media costs] was that we did not have the financial reserves that Bill Clinton did, so he could define me in his TV ads. . . . And since we had no capacity to respond to that, I was defined by someone else's ads.

Finally, early money is important in meeting early cash flow demands. Not only does it allow candidates to fund the initial contests in Iowa and New Hampshire adequately, it also gives them the luxury of starting early to build effective campaign organizations in states whose primaries and caucuses come shortly thereafter. For example, Walter Mondale in 1984 had organizations in place in most states long before Gary Hart came to national attention in the New Hampshire primary, and these helped Mondale to withstand Hart's challenge.

The need for sustained money

Although early money is especially important, maintaining a flow of sufficient funds throughout the season is equally crucial. Adequate resources have been important in meeting the enormous cash flow demands imposed by Super Tuesday and the primaries immediately following it, demands magnified by the intensity of the contest itself, with its premium on early wins and its widely acknowledged strategic imperative of knocking out the opposition quickly. The increased frontloading of the 1996 electoral calendar accentuates these demands.

The cash demands of February through April are so great that competitive candidates generally cannot raise money as fast as they need to spend it during this period, even if they are carefully selective in choosing events to contest. Gone are the days (if ever there were such) when a financially insecure candidate could parlay the momentum of early political successes into funds adequate to meet the cash flow requirements of midseason. This is especially true for less-well-known candidates. Electoral "bumps" from early victories are usually not fully matched by financial bumps, and perhaps less so now than ever.[3] This is all the more important because, according to Michael Malbin (looking at 1976–84), "Candidates spent their money much more quickly, proportionately, than delegates were chosen."[4]

A classic example was Gephardt in 1988, who failed to turn political momentum into cash, and, lacking cash, failed to sustain his political momentum. Although there is some dispute over whether the failure was in fundraising itself or in money management,[5] the bottom line was that he had a grossly inadequate cash position when he needed it. According to his campaign manager, William Carrick, "There wasn't enough time to collect the money bump" (Runkel 1989, p. 174). This was a crucial factor in the view of commentator Larry Eichel, who suggested that even though Gephardt had a budding populist constituency and momentum from his victory in Iowa, "What he did not have was money. Without it, he could not get his television commercials on the air in sufficient numbers to make an impact. And so, as the pace of the fight quickened, Gephardt became all but invisible. . . .With money, he could have been a contender; without it, he became a footnote" (Runkel 1989, p. 170).

Put simply: those candidates who can build large cash reserves, and who therefore have money available at those peak times when the demands for cash are greatest, have an enormous advantage over those whose financial base is less secure and less predictable. Furthermore, since candidate-attended events are an important source of money for many campaigns, staging them during the peak primary season puts serious burdens not only on scarce staff resources, but especially on the candidate's own time – the campaign's scarcest resource of all.

As shown by the examples of Bush and Dukakis in 1988, and Clinton in 1992, it is not necessary to have every penny in the bank by January 1. A campaign need only have a large cushion, so that it can proceed with confidence throughout the opening phases, raising money as it goes along to keep part of that cushion there. One obvious key is the ability to conserve the money raised early. Robertson, for example, lacked this key. He raised large sums of money before the season began, but much of this was plowed back into direct mail fund raising costs, and he was left with no reserve cushion when the season opened.

Money is crucial not only for the contests on the event calendar, but also for the ongoing national expenses of a campaign, including the costs of a national headquarters staff, the creative costs of advertising, and the candidate-support operation associated with the campaign on the road. Early money, followed by an adequate cash flow during the first few caucus and primary months, enables a campaign organization to perform its functions creatively and effectively. Medium-term planning becomes possible, and the various segments of the campaign organization can function with less debilitating zero-sum financial rivalry. As Anthony Corrado puts it, "Early money creates the opportunity to be pro-active."[6]

Moreover, the *appearance* of being able to maintain a first-class national campaign operation translates into media assessments of the campaign's chances. One of the surest signs a campaign is beginning to fail is when it begins to lay off staff: the press notices this instantly and trumpets it widely to the immediate disadvantage of the candidacy. Maintaining a steady cash flow to the national staff, therefore, can be almost as important as meeting peak demands from the states.

In addition, adequate cash reserves from early money can help candidates to survive serious setbacks and still continue their campaign. Candidacies frequently encounter reverses – an embarrassing revelation, a less-than-expected showing in a closely watched caucus or primary, a damaging misstatement, or a telling attack by an opponent. Such reverses can snowball politically, and can also lead to financial catastrophe, proving fatal to those candidates who lack the cash reserves to weather the storm (or lack strong sustaining political constituencies that are willing to ignore the lapse).

Virtually every candidacy will face some setback, and the ability to sustain, or even *regain*, momentum may be nearly as important strategically as the ability to create momentum in the first place. Political science has justifiably paid a good deal of attention to the concept of momentum (Bartels 1988; Aldrich 1980), but "staying power" is also important. Cash reserves can buy this staying power for a candidacy, enabling the candidate to endure periods of misfortune in a protracted and complex contest that strongly rewards the mere ability to outlast. As Corrado put it, "In 1984 with Mondale, we knew that as long as we could raise money and stay in the race we could wear Hart down. Because we had a strong financial base, we knew we had the resources to stay in the race."[7] And as Abramson, Aldrich, and Rhode observed, the winners in 1988 had the "best organized and best financed campaign organizations in their respective parties. . . . They had the resources to withstand defeats" (1990, p. 25). Clinton's financial base and his cash reserves certainly helped him survive the Gennifer Flowers scandal in 1992.

Finally, superior financial resources, often based on early money, bring with them enormous psychological advantages. When the candidate has to waste time begging for money instead of putting out a message; when the staff worries about layoffs, pay cuts, and missed paychecks; when excellent political opportunities have to be missed for lack of resources; when serious attacks cannot be countered for the same reason; and when there is a debilitating atmosphere of financial uncertainty hanging over the whole campaign – then morale suffers, and with it the entire effort. A financial cushion brings with it a fruitful sense of efficacy, mastery, and advantage: the campaign will go on; the message will get out. Money, especially early money, shortens the odds, and its sources therefore become a legitimate ground for political inquiry.

The little-studied role of the individual contributor

Where does this money come from? In presidential nomination finance, the generating source of almost all money is the individual contributor. Not only do individual contributions constitute the largest single portion of campaign receipts, but both federal matching funds and bank loans guaranteed by those funds are a direct function of individual contributions. Political Action Committees (PACs) do not play a central role in presidential nomination finance – in sharp contrast to the case of congressional campaign finance.

Since federal law limits the size of contributions to presidential nomination candidates to no more than $1,000, their campaigns, to be competitive, must receive contributions from tens of thousands of individuals. Massive fundraising efforts therefore characterize every major nomination campaign.

It is difficult to determine exactly how many individuals make contributions to presidential campaigns, since records are kept by contribution not by contributor, since many individuals make more than one contribution to a single candidate, and since many make contributions to more than one candidate. It is safe to say, however, that over a half million individuals made contributions totaling $143 million to presidential candidates during the 1988 nomination process, and more than a quarter million made contributions totaling $82 million during the 1992 process.[8]

Even though individuals dominate nomination finance, far more attention has been paid to the intermediaries (such as PACs and parties) that collect monies from individuals and distribute them to candidates (especially candidates for Congress) than to the individual contributors themselves. A voluminous literature has arisen on PACs, detailing their structure, decision making, and contribution behavior (Biersack, Herrnson, and Wilcox 1994; Clawson, Neustadtl, and Bearden 1986; Eismeier and Pollock 1986, 1988; Evans 1988; Gopoian 1984; Latus 1984; Sabato 1984; Sorauf 1984, 1988; Wilcox 1988a, 1988b, 1989a; Wright 1985).

Another large literature explores the role of political parties in collecting and distributing funds (Cotter, Gibson, Bibby, and Huckshorn 1984; Herrnson 1988, 1989; Jacobson 1980, 1986). Even a fair amount of attention has been paid to the candidates themselves, both as a source of funds to their own campaign (Wilcox 1988c) and as contributors to other candidates via their campaign committees or personal PACs (Corrado 1992; Wilcox 1989b; Wilcox and Genest 1991).

Despite this important literature on PACs and parties, little has been published about individual contributors based on systematic behavioral and attitudinal investigation. There are very important aggregate studies of individual contributors, most notably Alexander's quadrennial series (Alexander 1971, 1976, 1979, 1983; Alexander and Bauer 1991; Alexander and Corrado 1994). There are also good journalistic accounts of the role of contributors in campaign finance (e.g., Babcock and Morin 1992a, 1992b; Jackson 1988; Werth 1988), but surprisingly little research has been done on the methods of soliciting individual contributors, on contributor motivations, and especially on the interrelated decisions of contributors and campaigns.

Some scholars (Dunn 1965; Jones and Miller 1985; Sorauf 1988, 1992) have used data from the National Election Studies conducted by the Center for Political Studies at the University of Michigan to describe those who give money to political causes, and these studies have been fruitful. For example, Sorauf (1992) reported that political contributors in 1990 had higher levels of education, occupational prestige, and income than other Americans (and indeed than other party activists), and were more interested in politics than nonactivists. Jones and Miller (1985) found differences among those who gave to candidates, PACs, and party committees.

Others have indeed surveyed individuals who contributed to candidates, but most of the early studies focused on contributors to candidates in specific states (Berg, Eastland, and Jaffe 1981; Constantini and King 1982). In a later series of interesting studies, James Guth and John Green examined the political views of those who contributed to party committees and PACs, including PACs associated with presidential candidates (Guth and Green 1986, 1987, 1990, 1991; Green and Guth 1988; Green 1989). These authors explored the ideological and religious divisions among contributors, but they did not focus their research on the decision to contribute per se. Their work is therefore part of the larger literature on elite attitudes and behavior, but does not address directly questions of campaign finance.

Previous studies conducted in part by two of us (Brown, Hedges, and Powell 1980a, 1980b) examined the modes of participation, motivations, and ideological structure of contributors to presidential candidates in 1972, but these studies also focused on questions in the elite and political behavior literatures. Individual contributors remain the least studied element of the campaign finance system.

Serious money

This book is an attempt to fill the gap – at least partially. Our focus is on the individual contributor of what we call "serious money" – people whose contributions to a single candidate aggregate to at least $201 and are capped at $1,000. These individuals are considered by Congress to be sufficiently important to mandate publishing their names.

Contributors of serious money are an important group to study: well over half the money contributed in both 1988 and 1992 came from such individuals. In 1988, by our estimate, donors of serious money contributed more than 70% of the funds received from individuals by Bush, Dole, du Pont, Babbitt, Dukakis, Gephardt, and Gore. Since individual contributions are the generating source of almost all campaign funds, such contributors therefore played a sovereign role in the financial calculations of these seven candidates. In the case of Simon, contributors of serious money accounted for an estimated 58% of his total (from individuals), and in the case of Kemp, about 50% – still very important percentages.

Given the way Robertson compiled his Federal Election Commission (FEC) reports, it is more difficult to estimate the percentage of his money that was "serious." Richard Weinhold, who managed the Robertson direct mail effort in 1988, did indicate that a majority of contributors from Robertson's "1988 Team" eventually reached the $200 threshold.

Contributors of serious money played less of a role in the finances of Jackson, whose populist campaign was successful in raising large sums from numerous small contributors through churches as well as direct mail. We estimate that 21% of his total funds raised from individuals was serious money.

The same pattern held for 1992. More than 90% of Bush's funds, more than 80% of Clinton's, and more than 70% of Kerrey's were generated by donors of serious money. The percentages were less for Tsongas and Harkin, but still over half of their contributions came from this kind of donor. Only Buchanan (who raised about a third of his money from this source) and Brown (who refused to accept contributions over $100) based their campaigns primarily on successful efforts to mobilize small contributors.

Thus, although one of the main purposes of campaign finance reform legislation was to encourage candidates to concentrate more on small contributors in their fundraising activities, most candidates in 1988 and in 1992 based their campaigns primarily on serious money. Therefore, even though small contributors in the aggregate have a disproportionate impact on the bottom line through the federal match, contributors of serious money clearly play an essential and often dominant role in most nomination campaigns.

In this book, we examine these contributors of serious money, and especially the interrelated decisions by campaigns concerning whom to solicit, and by individuals concerning whether and to whom to give. Campaigns assess their resources and anticipate the decisions of potential contributors in deciding whom to solicit for contributions. Contributors then choose how to respond to each solicitation, and their decisions are influenced by their social and economic characteristics, their attitudes toward public questions, and their motivations for being involved in politics. To examine these decisions, we gathered information from several sources.

First, we conducted two surveys of presidential nomination contributors. Most of the data used in our analysis are based on a survey of 1,246 contributors of more than $200 to the 11 major 1988 presidential nomination candidates (Babbitt, Bush, Dole, du Pont, Dukakis, Gephardt, Gore, Jackson, Kemp, Robertson, and Simon).[9] The data were weighted to compensate for the increased likelihood of sampling a multiple contributor from the FEC list and also to reflect our estimate of the total distribution of contributors of serious money across the 11 candidates sampled.

The 1988 election was one of the best to study individual contributors to presidential candidates because it was the first in twenty years (and the first since the passage of the Federal Election Campaign Act) to be open in both parties, with each party fielding candidates who represented a wide range of ideological and constituency interests within that party.

We resurveyed our 1988 respondents after the end of the primary season in 1992.[10] Appendix I provides a description of each survey and the weighting schemes. Appendix II contains the survey items. Our purpose in this second survey was not to gather a representative sample of 1992 contributors, but rather to gather data that enable us to examine the decisions by campaigns in 1992 concerning whom to target, and the decisions by the contributors from 1988 concerning whether to give in 1992, and to whom. The 1988 data alone do not permit us to examine these decisions directly, for everyone in our survey was solicited and gave in 1988.

We make limited comparisons to an earlier survey of individual contributors of $100 or more to presidential candidates in 1972, the first year financial disclosure became law, and the last year before the current finance rules began to go into effect.[11] Given the rate of inflation, a $100 contribution in 1972 is roughly equivalent to a $200 contribution in 1988 or 1992.[12] Since the 1972 election predated federal financing of general election campaigns, the survey included contributors to both the nomination candidates and the general election candidates. For purposes of comparison, we therefore use for our analysis in this book a subsample of those who contributed during the preconvention season.

One important aspect of campaign finance is the decision by campaigns to target certain individuals for solicitation. The 1988 survey allowed us to profile the pool of individuals who regularly give to campaigns, a key factor in the targeting decisions made by campaign finance directors. The 1992 survey allowed us to examine the way the members of the 1988 pool were targeted by campaigns four years later. In order to gain a better understanding of targeting, we also conducted lengthy personal interviews with more than a dozen key campaign finance professionals from both parties who participated in the campaigns of 1988 and 1992. These interviews provided an in-depth, interpretative account of the decisions made by campaigns.

Finally, we rely upon aggregate data supplied by the FEC. These data are used primarily in the next chapter, where we trace the main contours of campaign finance activity from 1978 through 1992. This information provides one view of the ways campaigns respond to the rules that structure how contributions may be collected.

The structure of the argument

Since the decisions of potential individual campaign contributors have not been studied systematically before, there is not a well-established body of theory on which to build or a set of existing hypotheses to test. Although there is much excellent work on political participation, voting choice, public opinion, interest groups, and elites generally, theories in most cognate areas of study have been developed to answer questions other than those we wish to address.

Many authors in a wide variety of areas of political science have focused on the decisions of political actors (Arnold 1990; Clausen 1973; Fenno 1973, 1978; Kingdon 1981). Jacobson and Kernell (1981) serve as an exemplar, and others have built upon their work to study the decisions of campaign finance actors. In the rational actor framework, candidates and contributors are seen as responding to the political environment in order to achieve their goals.

We begin with the assumption that the dynamics of campaign finance center around two sets of decisions: the strategic decisions of campaigns to target potential contributors, and the personal decisions by those targeted to give or not to give.

Needless to say, these decisions are logically interrelated, since candidates will base their approach to potential donors on general assessments of why people give and on specific assessments of which people will actually give to their own campaigns. Furthermore, people's decisions to give will depend in part on which campaigns approach them and how the approaches are made. It is therefore important to examine the dynamics of campaign finance from both sides of the equation, and we attempt to do so in this book.

The starting point of our analysis, however, must be the campaign, since that is where the initiative lies. Very few people contribute without being asked; they give in response to a specific solicitation by a campaign (Sorauf 1992). How campaigns decide to raise money, therefore, is where our analysis must logically begin.

Campaign finance decisions, first of all, are shaped by two important constraints that each campaign must take as givens: the existing regulatory environment, and the existing pool of potential contributors. We therefore begin our analysis with a discussion of these two elements of the strategic environment.

The following chapter presents the regulatory environment within which campaign decisions are made – the rules of campaign finance and the apparent consequences of those rules as illustrated by aggregate FEC data for the years following their adoption. Since these rules were developed with reform objectives in mind, a discussion of the rules and their apparent implications cannot ignore reform objectives and the reform consequences of the rules. Our emphasis in Chapter 2, however, is on the strategic consequences of the rules in terms of how they shape campaign decisions.

Our data show that the vast majority of those who give to presidential nomination candidates in any particular election cycle have given at least occasionally in the past and are therefore part of an existing pool of potential contributors. Thus, the second constraint faced by a campaign is this pool of potential contributors – which constitutes the principal playing field upon which the finance game unfolds. Chapter 3 examines this pool. It begins by establishing the pool's existence and its stability over time, despite the changing constellations of candidates. We also discuss the dynamics of recruitment of members to the pool. Finally, to define the nature of this strategic playing field in more precise terms, we describe the demographic features, political activities, and motives of those who make it up, and how little these factors have changed over the last twenty years.

With the regulatory environment and the pool of contributors as constraints, campaigns must then decide how to approach potential donors, mostly in the existing pool, sometimes outside of it, to ask them for a contribution. There are several options available, but over time campaigns have decided to raise the bulk of their money through two basic methods of solicitation: direct mail and personal networking. In Chapter 4 we discuss in qualitative terms these two very important tools and the two very different fundraising cultures built around them. Then, using the results of our surveys, we explicate them quantitatively.

We also demonstrate in Chapter 4 that the two fundraising cultures do not exist merely as a result of technical developments in fundraising, but rather are grounded in the different underlying motives that contributors give for participating in politics. In showing this, we explore the very strong and interesting relationships between the way in which contributors were successfully approached in 1988, and their political motivations.

Given the rules, the pool of contributors, and the instruments for reaching them, campaigns must then decide whom to target and by what method of approach. In making such decisions, each campaign rationally must assess the political resources of its candidate and build a strategy to take maximum advantage of them. These resources are explored in Chapter 5. Although every candidate will have his or her own unique set of resources, we identify several types that were important in 1988 and probably will remain so in the future.

The first candidate resource analyzed is the ability to create or activate the financial networks within that candidate's home state. Sitting governors and some senators have this resource readily available to them; many representatives to a lesser extent do also. The larger the state and the more politically powerful the candidate, the more important this resource is.

In addition, some candidates have the resources to tap national networks of contributors who typically are best approached through personal contact. Although there are many kinds of such resources, we analyze three historically important ones that have been used successfully by recent candidates: traditional ties to national party activists, positions of congressional leadership, and social identity. These resources are mobilized largely by using the method of personal solicitation to activate parts of the contributing pool or to attract new members to the pool. This list is not exhaustive, but it does include the principal types of national networks mobilized in 1988 and 1992.

Finally, a very important resource is a candidate's ideological position, which enables a campaign to tap like-minded members of the existing pool or to recruit new members to the pool. This is a given resource in any campaign, although a candidate over time may have some limited flexibility in terms of positioning on the ideological spectrum. Candidates who are ideologically extreme generally rely upon direct mail and telemarketing to exploit this resource.

Thus in Chapter 5 we examine how the campaigns in 1988, given the political resources of their candidates, succeeded in building their financial constituencies by identifying which segments of the pool they were successful in tapping. Our data do not enable us to examine for 1988 which segments of the pool they attempted to tap, since we have only a sample of those who gave, not of those who were asked to give.

With these points established, we show in Chapter 6, using the unique set of data from the panel study, which pool members were asked to contribute and which, among those asked, actually contributed. The data enable us to identify and predict which members of the 1988 pool were asked to give by impersonal methods of solicitation in 1992, and which were approached through personal contact. We can also predict, among those asked by each method, which ones actually gave. To make these predictions, we use measures developed in the previous chapters, including measures of contribution patterns, patterns of political campaign activity, motivation, and ideology. In addition to identifying who was asked to contribute in 1992, we can identify who was asked to solicit contributions from others – and who then did solicit others to contribute. These results also enable us to shed light on the related questions of why certain kinds of people are asked to give and solicit, and why they do give and solicit.

Chapter 7 presents our conclusions, the theoretical implications of our findings, and our recommendations for further study.

2. The regulatory environment

The strategic calculations of political campaigns logically begin with the rules of play. In the case of presidential nomination campaigns, those rules are set by national parties, state legislatures, Congress, and the Supreme Court. These four noncoordinated rule-making bodies have produced a complex and evolving strategic environment characterized in recent election cycles by many primary contests, ever-changing regulations for selecting delegates, and an increasingly front-loaded event calendar. An important and relatively stable part of this strategic environment has been the congressionally and judicially mandated set of rules governing nomination campaign finance.

These finance rules have been in place since 1976 and fully implemented in four election cycles, starting in 1980. They limit the amount of money individuals can give to candidates and the amount candidates can spend nationally and in each state. They also provide matching funds for individual contributions, which enhances the ability of candidates to raise large sums from many small donations. This legal framework thus creates a regulatory structure within which the strategic calculations of nomination campaigns must be made. It also creates the environment in which individual decisions to contribute are taken. In doing so, it strongly influences the interactions between the campaigns and those individuals who may wish to participate. This chapter explores the impact of these rules on presidential nomination finance.

The regulation of contributions: FECA

In 1971 Congress passed the Federal Election Campaign Act (FECA), which provided for the disclosure of contributions and expenditures in the quest for national office. The law took effect after April 7, 1972, and required that candidates and party committees provide the General Accounting Office (GAO) with the names and addresses of all contributors whose gifts aggregated to more than $100. It was from this population of contributors that a sample was drawn to obtain the survey data used in this book for the 1972 elections. (See Brown, Hedges, and Powell, 1980a.) Though modified, disclosure rules remain a central feature of presidential nomination finance.

In response to the revelations of Watergate, Congress in 1974 passed important amendments to the FECA that radically transformed the financing of presidential prenomination campaigns. The law was subsequently modified by the Supreme Court in *Buckley* v. *Valeo* in 1976. The resulting set of regulations, enforced by the specially created Federal Election Commission (FEC), has several important provisions that affect decisions by campaigns and contributors.

First, the size of contributions by individuals, interest groups, and candidates is limited. Individuals can contribute no more than $1,000 to any candidate in any election.[1] Interest groups, through PACs, can contribute no more than $5,000 to candidates for the nomination. Candidates themselves, if they accept matching funds, can contribute only $50,000 of their own money to fund their campaigns, although they can spend all they want on their own campaign if they do not accept matching funds. These limits, set in 1974, have not increased with inflation, and so a $1,000 contribution made in 1974 would buy roughly twice as much in that election cycle as a gift of the same amount would buy in 1988. To enforce these limits, campaigns must report to the FEC the names and addresses of all contributors whose gifts aggregate to more than $200.

Second, during the prenomination campaign candidates can qualify for public matching funds by raising $100,000 in individual contributions in amounts of $250 or less, with $5,000 coming from each of twenty states. Once a candidate has met these criteria, up to $250 of the total contributions an individual makes to that candidate's campaign may be matched by money from the federal fund. There is an overall cap on total matching funds that any candidate may receive in a presidential election. The limit, which is indexed to the Consumer Price Index, was approximately $11.5 million in 1988 and $13.8 million in 1992. Ronald Reagan in 1984 was the only candidate ever to accept the maximum possible matching funds.

The match is terminated if on two consecutive primary days a candidate fails to receive at least 10% of the vote in at least one primary election that the candidate seriously contests. If a candidate does not contest a primary, he or she must certify this to the FEC in advance. A candidate may requalify for funds by receiving 20% of the vote in a subsequent primary. No candidate in 1988 or 1992 lost and then again qualified for matching funds, although Jesse Jackson did so in 1984. The lurking threat of forfeiting the match, however, can influence a candidate's decision to abandon the race.[2]

For candidates who accept matching funds, there are spending limits for each state. These limits, which are routinely circumvented by the endless creativity of campaigns (Wilcox 1991), are not directly relevant to our study of contributors. Candidates who accept matching funds must also agree to a national limit for the entire campaign. In 1988, this limit was approximately $23 million, with an additional $4.6 million allowed for spending on fundraising and legal fees. In 1992, the national limit was $27.6 million, with an additional $5.5 million allowed for money spent on fundraising and legal fees. Successful campaigns generally raise money equal to this spending limit, so the figure constitutes the initial goal of campaign strategic financial plans.

Exemptions in the law create a variety of opportunities for campaigns to raise money beyond the national totals. These include candidate PACs,[3] tax-exempt foundations, independent expenditures, and delegate committees. Although the rules permitting "soft money" contributions allow individuals to give large amounts during the general election campaign, they do not affect nomination finance. These exemptions are not so extensive in their use as to alter the basic reliance of nomination campaigns on the individual contributor examined in this study.

Consequences of the FECA

The structure of finance

The rules embodied in the FECA shape the structure of nomination finance and help determine the configuration of sources from which a campaign receives its money. Table 2.1 presents the sources of receipts for each of the principal candidates for the two major parties in each election cycle. Nearly all receipts for presidential prenomination candidates have come from three sources: individual contributions, federal matching funds based on those individual contributions, and loans advanced against those matching funds. Individual contributions are by far the most important source of campaign receipts and are directly responsible for the other two main sources. Therefore individual contributions account for at least 95% of all of the funding for the campaigns of every candidate since 1980.

The matching funds provided by the FECA rules have played an important role in financing presidential campaigns. Only once during this period has a major candidate chosen to forgo federal matching funds in order to avoid the attendant limits on campaign spending.[4] Despite Reagan's expressed disapproval of matching funds, his campaigns never publicly dis-

Table 2.1. *Sources of receipts: 1980–92 (in thousands)*

	Individuals	Matching funds	Loans	PACs & parties
1980				
Carter	13,000	5,052	0	500
Kennedy	7,761	3,863	2,653	240
Anderson	3,910	2,680	175	24
Bush	10,929	5,716	4,467	131
Connally	11,784	0	578	210
Crane	3,480	1,755	40	2
Dole	902	446	50	46
Reagan	13,886	7,193	5,513	288
1984				
Glenn	6,683	3,325	2,655	398
Hart	8,919	5,328	7,720	9
Jackson	5,139	3,061	637	31
Mondale	17,415	9,495	7,672	1
Reagan	16,485	10,100	200	131
1988				
Babbitt	2,265	1,079	905	1
Dukakis	19,401	9,040	0	9
Gephardt	6,313	2,896	2,528	661
Gore	8,015	3,853	1,560	517
Jackson	12,282	7,608	5,169	47
Simon	6,147	3,603	3,037	300
Bush	22,567	8,393	50	673
Dole	17,430	7,618	0	849
du Pont	5,502	2,551	828	0
Kemp	10,568	5,877	3,300	65
Robertson	20,637	9,691	9,553	0
1992				
Brown	4,560	857	600	0
Clinton	14,179	4,240	1,900	3
Harkin	2.780	1,734	0	330
Kerrey	3,457	1,784	10	280
Tsongas	4,775	1,443	550	2
Buchanan	4,817	2,877	0	27
Bush	23,969	6,785	0	36

Source: FEC Reports on Financial Activity: Final Presidential Reports 1980, 1984, 1988, and final press release for 1992.

cussed the possibility of refusing them. In 1988, Robertson announced that he was considering doing so. His campaign, however, secured loans against their availability and he eventually accepted them to make payments on those loans, even though for a while he suggested that he might choose to return the matching funds he had accepted.

Bank loans secured against federal matching funds are valuable ways for cash-poor campaigns to capitalize on their momentum from early victories. Had Hart not been able to borrow nearly $6 million in 1984 after his upset victory over Mondale in New Hampshire, his campaign would surely have faltered, for it took time for his victory to translate into increased levels of individual contributions. Loans can also help campaigns spend their matching funds before they are released by the FEC. In 1988, Babbitt, Simon, du Pont, Kemp, and Gephardt borrowed against the match prior to January 1 to get their campaigns off the ground. In 1992, Clinton used lines of credit to augment cash flows in anticipation of matching funds. The existence of the match, and its solid guarantee of cash receivable at a future date, makes loans secured in that fashion a safe bet for the lender. Thus the FECA has created an environment where loans are an active and viable part of campaign finance.

Party committees and PACs do not provide substantial direct funds to presidential campaigns. Because parties seldom take sides in primary contests, they contribute only after the winner is selected. Some candidates eschew PAC contributions as a matter of principle, but even among those who accept PAC money the conjunction of the cap on PAC contributions, the relatively small number of these committees, and their general reluctance to give in primary elections means that PACs are a minor factor in presidential nomination finance.

Although PACs do not play an important direct role in financing presidential campaigns, the interest groups they represent are more important than the data in Table 2.1 indicate. First, PACs provide a significant source of the funds raised by the special candidate PACs – the political action committees that many presidential hopefuls form prior to their official declaration of candidacy. Second, PACs are the principal source of independent expenditures. Third, networks of PAC contributors, including corporate executives, provide a major source of individual contributions for some presidential candidates. Herbert Alexander (1989), in one of his valuable studies of presidential campaign finance, noted that Dukakis was able to solicit ten to twenty contributions from executives of specific companies in Massachusetts, who provided far more total funds than a simple PAC contribution would have. Also, in 1992, both Bush and Clinton received substantial amounts of money from a number of executives from within single corporations (Devroy and Babcock 1992). Thus interest groups do provide substantial amounts of funds to candidates, but the mechanism of these financial transfers is usually the individual contribution and not the PAC.

Large numbers

The number of contributors a successful campaign must reach is large. The most important consequence of the FECA reforms has been and remains the need for campaigns to raise money from many more individuals than in earlier years. Campaign strategists, in identifying and soliciting contributors, are severely constrained by the contribution limits of the FECA, which prevent wealthy individuals from making huge gifts. Alexander (1971, 1976) reports that in the two elections prior to the 1974 FECA amendments, the campaigns of the major candidates all received much, and in many cases most, of their revenues from very large contributions. This was true even of candidates who made strong value-laden or ideological appeals, such as Eugene McCarthy in 1968, who, Alexander reports, raised $2.5 million from fifty contributors. George McGovern in 1972 also received a substantial portion of his total funds from contributions and loans made by a few individuals.

With a limit of $1,000 per person, it can take hundreds of contributors to equal the total contributed by one of those large, prereform donors. As Democratic fundraiser Carol Hassamen put it, "Used to be, you'd get a dozen people in the room and come up with half a million dollars for sure. Now if you get $25,000 you're doing great."[5]

In 1988, Bush raised more than $22 million in individual contributions, and Dukakis raised more than $19 million. To achieve these totals, each campaign successfully solicited more than 25,000 individual contributors. Candidates from the ideological wings of their parties, such as Robertson and Jackson, rely primarily on much smaller donations, and so must identify many more potential contributors. In 1992, even with the match, to raise the maximum allowable expenditures from direct mail, more than a quarter of a million contributors averaging $50 apiece would be needed. Thus the FECA created the need for candidates to broaden greatly their fundraising base.

In addition, the minimum number of large contributors needed to raise the maximum amount of expendable money increases every year because the expenditure totals are indexed to inflation, while the size of the maximum contribution is not. In 1980 a candidate needed to tap approximately 10,000 contributors of $1,000 to raise (with the match) the maximum he or she could spend; in 1992, a candidate needed to tap 25,000 such contributors. For any given size of average contribution, a candidate, to raise the equivalent amount of spending power, needs more than twice as many contributors today as when the rules went into effect, and that number will keep increasing. Although inflation has reduced the real dollar value of a contribution of a given amount, thereby increasing the number of individuals willing to make such a contribution, nevertheless it still takes more effort to identify and reach this larger number of donors. Hence, the FECA rules, combined with the reality of inflation, continually tend to expand the number of contributors needed to finance a successful campaign – and therefore expand the campaign's effort needed to reach them.

Early starts

One strategic consequence of the need to develop an ever-larger base of contributors is the need to start early. This requirement is made all the more urgent by the cash demands associated with event-calendar front-loading and the publicity advantages of building a "financial front-runner" position. For such reasons, and the fact that professional campaign managers tend to follow the example of past campaigns, it has become common for candidates to begin to organize and raise money early in the election cycle, often two or more years before the start of the primary season.

The timing of candidate fundraising is presented in Table 2.2, which shows total net receipts for each candidate through the end of May of the election year. These totals include monies raised for compliance costs and other accounts, so the totals occasionally exceed the legal maximum for direct campaign spending. For most candidates fundraising continues after this date, but by then all primaries and caucuses are over.

In the 1980 election cycle, no major candidate raised 35% of his funds before the start of the election year. Only Mondale in the 1984 cycle raised a substantial percentage of his funds in the year before the official start of the campaign. In 1988, Dukakis, Bush, Dole, Kemp, and Robertson each raised more than 35% of his funds before the start of the election year, with Bush, Dole, and Kemp each raising more than half.[6] In 1992, candidates began their fundraising later than usual. Democratic candidates spent months debating the wisdom of challenging a popular George Bush before finally announcing their candidacies, and the Bush campaign saw no reason to begin early fundraising, since the incumbent president was exceedingly popular in the

Table 2.2. *The dynamics of total fundraising: 1980–92 (in millions)*

	Sept.	Dec.	Jan.	Feb.	Mar.	Apr.	May
1980							
Carter	2.42	5.75	8.53	11.13	12.98	14.71	16.46
Kennedy	0	3.89	6.11	7.67	9.49	11.06	13.62
Anderson	0.29	.51	.66	1.58	4.52	6.87	6.96
Bush	2.43	4.46	6.56	9.41	14.47	18.68	20.51
Connally	4.30	9.16	10.01	11.64	12.66	12.85	12.99
Crane	2.94	3.27	4.11	4.51	4.95	5.19	5.22
Dole	.51	.78	1.27	1.35	1.43	1.43	1.47
Reagan	2.79	7.21	12.02	16.36	18.91	21.55	24.49
1984							
Glenn	4.25	6.42	9.01	12.45	13.15	13.36	13.47
Hart	1.55	1.88	2.83	3.82	12.05	16.41	19.92
Jackson	0	0.35	0.76	1.57	1.94	3.61	5.55
Mondale	6.95	11.45	16.48	18.25	23.01	25.92	29.82
Reagan	0	3.77	4.81	10.85	16.43	23.17	26.25
1988							
Babbitt	1.92	2.45	3.57	3.93	4.01	4.11	4.24
Dukakis	7.74	10.37	14.69	17.56	20.99	24.43	27.89
Gephardt	3.46	5.90	8.08	9.57	11.66	12.16	12.30
Gore	2.70	3.94	5.99	7.53	10.94	12.37	12.83
Jackson	1.04	1.40	2.68	4.15	7.42	12.28	16.93
Simon	2.04	6.06	9.00	10.68	11.62	11.92	12.21
Bush	12.73	19.06	26.29	27.75	29.92	32.06	32.58
Dole	7.96	14.32	21.09	23.12	25.52	26.88	27.31
du Pont	3.43	5.54	8.23	8.68	8.81	9.09	9.11
Kemp	6.30	10.21	15.93	17.55	18.20	18.99	19.44
Robertson	11.74	16.41	29.70	34.69	37.01	38.10	38.60
1992							
Brown	0.05	0.52	0.94	1.46	3.41	6.02	6.02
Clinton	0.20	3.29	5.47	8.61	12.87	16.64	20.33
Harkin	0.71	2.17	3.56	4.61	4.75	4.85	4.85
Kerrey	0.22	1.91	3.26	4.92	5.26	5.40	5.53
Tsongas	0.79	1.31	1.88	3.75	6.23	6.67	6.77
Buchanan	0	0.71	1.72	4.22	6.16	7.05	7.77
Bush	0	9.96	14.17	18.97	23.63	27.08	30.95

Figures represent total cumulative receipts of campaign committees for each reporting period.
Source: FEC Reports of Financial Activity: Final Presidential Reports 1980, 1984, 1988, and monthly press releases for 1991 and 1992.

aftermath of the Persian Gulf War. It seems likely that the 1992 election was an aberration, however, for some Republican presidential candidates formed PACs in 1994, in part to help identify potential contributors for the 1996 campaign, and many had already raised substantial funds by 1995.

Not only does the FECA framework lead candidates to early fundraising, it also makes it more difficult for candidates to enter the race late. Although a good deal of media attention during the 1988 campaign was devoted to speculation about the possible entry of New York Governor Mario Cuomo in the midst of the campaign, in fact the implications of the campaign finance law would have made such an entry extremely difficult. Robert Kennedy was able to enter the 1968 presidential primaries late and raise $11 million in 11 weeks, mostly in large contributions, but in 1988 Cuomo would have been able to accept only $1,000 from any single contributor, and he would have needed a list of 8,800 individual contributors willing to "go the limit" to match Kennedy's fundraising success, even with matching funds. He would have needed twice as many contributors to raise as much as Kennedy in real terms. Even if Cuomo had somehow managed to raise such large sums quickly, he would still have trailed Dukakis in total receipts.

The need to raise substantial sums early in the election cycle, long before many contributors have begun to focus on the election, has meant that candidates frequently rely on supporters in their home state or congressional district for their earliest receipts. As we show in Chapter 5, sitting governors from large states are especially able to raise large sums early in the campaign. Whether or not a candidate begins with a strong in-state effort, the FECA framework requirement drives all campaigns into national fundraising before January 1, the earliest date on which matching funds can be allotted, because any candidate who desires matching funds must raise money in at least twenty states.

Ideological candidates and moderate candidates

The FECA reforms were intended to encourage campaigns to rely on small contributions from many donors. Matching funds make it easier for candidates to finance their campaigns through these small donations, for they double the value of any contribution of $250 or less. Because larger contributions are only partially matched, the system benefits those candidates who rely on smaller donations relative to those who rely on larger ones.

These features of the FECA framework had an important impact on the role of direct mail in presidential nomination finance. As discussed in

Chapter 4, a successful mailing can have a substantially lower return rate with the match than without it, which means that the match can substantially increase the reach of direct mail prospecting. In addition, responses to direct mail appeals tend to be in small dollar amounts, so most are fully matchable. The match therefore has been a significant factor in the use of direct mail for presidential nomination fundraising.

Direct mail and other impersonal techniques tend to be most successful for candidates who appeal to voters on the basis of values, which most often are expressed in ideological terms.[7] As Alexander puts it, "Generally, direct mail is lucrative for candidates who appeal to strong emotions in the voters, and less successful for low-key centrist politicians."[8] This means that candidates at the ends of the ideological spectrum are probably advantaged significantly by the FECA framework. The development of cheap and accessible computer technology and of a network of consultants to use that technology has allowed candidates to mail solicitations to potential donors whose names appear on lists that reveal their likely ideology. The existence of matching funds allowed candidates such as Pat Robertson in 1988 and Patrick Buchanan in 1992 to fund sizable campaigns through small donations from their supporters, many of whom in our survey locate themselves at the ends of the ideological scale. They also helped Jerry Brown to conduct a campaign in 1992 that accepted only small contributions frequently sent in response to his campaign's "800 number." Most of the contributions to these candidates were doubled in value by the match.

Campaign finance professionals disagree as to whether the elimination of matching funds would severely impede the ability of candidates at the ends of the ideological spectrum to raise funds through mail. Scott McKenzie, who directed the mail operations for Kemp and Buchanan, argues that without the match such campaigns would find it difficult to raise enough money to compete effectively. Robertson fundraiser Richard Weinhold concludes, however, that Robertson could have raised far more money during the campaign than he did, for he was ultimately constrained by the overall spending cap. Hal Malchow, who directed the Kerrey direct mail effort in 1992, notes that many Senate candidates do quite well with direct mail and telemarketing without matching funds. Clearly, however, contribution limits and matching funds do help candidates from the ends of the ideological spectrum who employ value-laden messages. Thus the FECA framework tends to enhance the reach of direct mail, and direct mail, in turn, has the potential for being used most effectively by candidates who stir emotion.

In contrast, the $1,000 limit disadvantages candidates whose contributors would be willing to make larger contributions. In the 1988 campaign, Bush,

Dole, Dukakis, Gephardt, and Gore all received substantial proportions of their funds in $1,000 contributions, and in 1992 the Bush campaign relied almost entirely on these large gifts. Many of the contributors to these candidates would probably have given more if there were no contribution limits, or if those limits were set to a higher value.

If the limit on individual contributions had been indexed to inflation in 1974, those contributors would have been able to give nearly $2,200 to their preferred candidate in 1988 and $2,500 in 1992, and the campaigns of these candidates would have raised money more quickly and cheaply. These candidates were also disadvantaged by the limitation of matching funds to the first $250 contributed by any individual. If the matching fund limit of $250 had kept up with inflation since 1974, then the first $550 of each gift would have been matched by the government in 1988, and the first $625 would have been matched in 1992. This would have provided significantly more revenue for Bush, Dole, Dukakis, Gephardt, and Gore. As discussed in Chapter 5, these candidates were widely perceived by contributors as ideologically moderate.

It is difficult to overstate the impact of the $1,000 limit on the fundraising culture, and especially on personal-network fundraising. Before the FECA framework was established, the principal source of money for most candidates in both parties was the personally solicited contributor of truly large amounts, but the $1,000 limit changed all this. Not only did the FECA framework encourage direct mail, but it also initially discouraged the traditional personal-network form of fundraising. Professional fundraisers, used to raising six-digit sums with a single telephone call, now could get, at most, only low four-digit sums per call, and so they exhausted their lists of contacts before obtaining a fraction of the money they formerly had raised.

At first glance, the new math was discouraging. Theoretically, it took a thousand contributions to raise a million dollars, and even though in practice (through the use of spouses and children) this number might be smaller, still not a lot of fundraisers could easily touch enough people to raise the needed funds. Therefore, although personal networking continued to be an important source of funds in 1976 and 1980, many candidates were forced to look to more broad-based methods to aggregate small contributions over a large pool of contributors, and the role of personally solicited funds was seriously downgraded.

Highly organized broad-based personal-contact solicitation, however, began a major comeback with Mondale in 1984: he was able to raise sizable portions of his total funds through personal-contact solicitation (and its attendant fundraising events); by 1988 this had become the preferred mode of solicitation for the winners in both parties, and a frequent form of successful solicitation for many losers, as well.

What made this all possible was the development of the pyramid. Given the mathematical constraints imposed by the $1,000 ceiling, successful personal solicitation campaigns came to rely on a very large number of people making the contacts, and this, in turn required a hierarchial structure, with central fundraisers identifying a large body of solicitors who recruited other solicitors as well as contributors. This often went down through several levels. As George Bush's 1988 fundraiser Fred Bush (no relation) described it, "The whole idea is working networks and cross-fertilization."[9] Sarah Epstein, a Dukakis fundraiser, described it as "wholesaling": "Retailing is getting on the phone and calling people you know. Wholesaling means you get names from those friends and get some of them to call for you."[10] Depending on the nature of the candidacy, the pyramid can be either steep and deep or broad and shallow, but in either case, it must be very large to raise competitive amounts of money. The several hundred successful top solicitors in a pyramid become very important political actors, crucial to the success of the entire effort. Thus the FECA framework created a wholly new fundraising culture to facilitate the raising of serious money through personal solicitations.

Large contributions

One result of the rise of personal-network pyramids was to make it possible for candidates to focus on the $1,000 contribution and ignore the advantages of raising fully matchable small contributions. An incentive to do so was provided by the pervasive inflation of the 1970s, which both eroded the value of matching funds and enhanced the ability of campaigns to raise $1,000 contributions. The value of the $250 match is now worth about $100 in 1974 terms, and the real cost of a $1,000 gift in 1992 is equivalent to the cost of a $400 contribution then.

Thus it is not surprising that many campaigns in 1988 and 1992 attempted to pursue larger contributions, accepting inflation-devalued matching funds as an almost incidental consequence. Table 2.3 shows the percentage of contributions to each major candidate in three size categories. In the 1980 and 1984 elections, only two candidates of the twelve who sought matching funds received more large contributions (over $750) than small ones (less than $500). In 1988 and 1992, nearly 40% of all candidates received more large than small contributions.

Table 2.3. *Individual Contributions by Size: 1980–92*

	$1–$499 (%)	$500–$749 (%)	$750–$1,000 (%)
1980			
Carter	32	18	50
Kennedy	59	11	31
Anderson	87	6	8
Bush	57	18	25
Connally	43	13	44
Crane	91	4	5
Dole	43	18	39
Reagan	59	11	30
1984			
Glenn	37	18	45
Hart	68	10	23
Jackson	86	6	8
Mondale	52	17	31
Reagan	63	9	29
1988			
Babbitt	35	12	54
Dukakis	37	20	42
Gephardt	43	19	38
Gore	44	17	39
Jackson	88	4	7
Simon	61	12	27
Bush	22	12	66
Dole	36	12	51
du Pont	45	14	40
Kemp	68	9	22
Robertson	89	3	8
1992			
Brown	100	0	0
Clinton	38	20	42
Harkin	73	8	19
Kerrey	41	16	43
Tsongas	60	13	26
Buchanan	83	6	12
Bush	9	9	82

Percentage of individual contributions by size of gift.
Source: FEC Reports of Financial Activity: Presidential Final Reports
1980, 1984, 1988, and final press release for 1992.

In 1988, Babbitt, Bush, Dole, du Pont, and Dukakis received more than 40% of their money in gifts of $750 or more, and Gephardt and Gore received nearly 40% of their funds from such gifts. Indeed, Bush in 1988 received nearly two-thirds of his funds from these large contributions, and in 1992 he raised more than 80% of his money from them. Bush, Dole, and Dukakis (and to a lesser extent Gephardt and Gore) primarily sought $1,000 contributions. Each candidate held $1,000-a-plate fundraisers and built personal networks that solicited large contributions. In 1988, both Dole and Dukakis collected over 7,000 gifts of $1000 each, and Bush received more than 16,000 of these maximum gifts (Alexander 1989).

This does not mean that all campaigns have given up on small contributions. Both Jackson and Robertson received nearly 90% of their contributions in 1988 in amounts of less than $500 – mostly in amounts smaller than $50, although resolicitation and repeated giving often meant that many individuals gave more than these amounts over the course of the campaign. Buchanan received the vast majority of his campaign funds in 1992 through small mail gifts, and Brown raised all of his $5 million that year in individual contributions from small gifts solicited through the mail or through his 800 number program. We are not seeing a general across-the-board trend to larger contributions; rather we observe a polarization of candidacies into those that seek (and find) large contributions, primarily through personal networks, and those that seek (and find) small contributions, primarily through mail and television techniques.

Conclusions

The regulatory structure described above and the strategic implications we have discussed affect the ways that campaigns identify and solicit contributors. Potential contributors in turn are also affected by the contribution limits, and by the need of campaigns to receive funds from many individuals. The rules provide a fundamental constraint on the behavior of campaigns and contributors.

These rules are not neutral. If the 1988 campaign had been conducted without the FECA limits, it seems likely that several of the moderate candidates could have raised even more money from fewer individuals making very large contributions. Their fundraising would have taken less time and left them more time to focus on the campaign. Without matching funds, the more ideologically extreme campaigns of Robertson and Jackson would have needed to contact even more potential contributors to maintain their revenues, and the yield of their direct mail solicitations would have been considerably worse. Whether or not the elimination of matching funds would severely impede the ability of candidates from the ideological wings of their parties to raise funds through the mail in the future, it remains very clear that contribution limits and matching funds help candidates who base their appeals on values.

The new rules have also been successful in opening up the process to new players. The current system, in sharp contrast to the previous one, has made it impossible for campaigns to be highly dependent on a handful of megacontributors, and to this extent a larger number of "smaller" players is necessary for financial success. Furthermore, this has been accomplished without appreciably narrowing the field of candidates: parties without an incumbent running for reelection have had full slates generally representing an ample ideological range within each party. This is important because the prereform system, for all its faults, encouraged a wide field of candidates to run: many potential contributors of megabucks were available throughout the ideological spectrum, and all it took was a few to fund a candidacy.

Despite the fact that the reforms have resulted in participation by many new contributors, however, caution is warranted in concluding that they have broadened the socioeconomic and demographic base of contributors. We show in Chapter 4 that many campaigns are coming to be highly dependent on a relatively small number of big-time, well-connected *solicitors* of money, so, in this sense, the "high rollers" have not been entirely removed from the process. In addition, as discussed in Chapter 3, contributors of serious money are effectively just as wealthy, well-educated, white, and male today as they were before the reform rules were implemented. To be sure, some candidates (like Robertson or Jackson) raised the bulk of their money from a numerically, though not ideologically, more broad-based and middle-class constituency than most other candidates did, and the rules, including the match, helped them do so. But overall, their ability to raise money from those of more modest means appears to have been as much a product of the ideological nature of their candidacies as of the finance rules themselves. Finally, there is some evidence that the reform rules have not expanded the geographic base of campaign contributions – and certainly not at the top end of the scale. The upper east coast, Florida, Texas, and California still dominate campaign finance as they did in 1972 before the current system went into effect.[11]

One important reform objective of the FECA legislation was to provide an opportunity for less-well-known and less-well-financed candidates to compete with the better-known and better-financed front-runners. This objective was to be achieved through the match and the spending limits.

The match was designed to extend the financial reach of lesser-known candidates by increasing their total funds early on when money was needed to buy name recognition and to deliver a message. Furthermore, the reforms created opportunities for lesser-known candidates to borrow against future matching funds and therefore spend money earlier than they might be able to otherwise.[12] Whether the match has really served to level the playing field, however, is open to dispute. Financial front-runners also receive more total funds from the match than do financial underdogs, thereby increasing the dollar gap between them. For example, matching funds provided Babbitt with nearly $750,000 in January 1988, which enabled him to continue his campaign in Iowa. But Dukakis received nearly $3.5 million at the same time. Similarly, although du Pont received over $2 million in January to make his case, Bush, Dole, and Robertson each received over $5.5 million.

Matching funds therefore may disproportionately help the underdog at the start of the campaign, since there is a general threshold of financial viability that the match may help the underdog surmount. The visibility bought with such "seed money" may also enable an initially unknown candidate to raise more money on his or her own behalf. But as the campaign unfolds, the match probably helps the front-runner, for the match expands the dollar advantage in total resources, a crucial factor in the current front-loaded game with its enormous cash flow demands.

There is one final consequence of the need for candidates to solicit quickly a large number of individuals who might be willing to give to their campaigns. Campaigns contact those who gave to presidential candidates in past elections because these individuals seem most likely to be motivated to contribute again. These past contributors constitute a pool of potential givers, and campaigns focus most of their attention in raising money on members of this pool. Direct mail professionals rent mailing lists from previous campaigns, and top solicitors reactivate personal networks that they tapped in previous campaigns for different candidates. We discuss these techniques more fully in Chapter 4. Even though candidates try to expand the pool by bringing in new contributors, campaigns have more success when they ask habitual givers for contributions than when they approach individuals who have never before given to a presidential candidate.

Thus the strategic environment, the rules, and the practices of campaigns have combined to create an expanding pool of campaign contributors that constitutes the central focus of campaign finance activity.

3. The contributor pool

Most donors of serious money to presidential nomination candidates come from an established pool of habitual givers, not from a body of mostly first-time contributors assembled on an ad hoc basis by different candidates each election cycle. As we saw in the preceding chapter, the size of the pool has generally grown election by election since the inception of the FECA rules. Yet even though there is defection from and especially recruitment to this pool, at any point in time the great majority of those who give serious money have contributed before and will do so again, though not necessarily in every election. In 1988, for example, 83% reported that they had contributed previously to a presidential candidate; 95% said they had previously made a political contribution of some kind.

This should not be surprising, since those who are motivated to contribute in one election will probably be motivated to do so the next time. All potential contributors must weigh the opportunity costs of making a cash contribution against an array of political, social, or material benefits that such a contribution might produce. Those who decided in the past that the benefits of contributing outweighed the costs are more likely to make a similar decision in the future than those who decided not to contribute in the past, or those who simply never considered doing so. Thus those who have a propensity to contribute in one election will probably have a propensity to do so next time.

Furthermore, such people are given every opportunity to act on their propensities and remain in the pool. Fundraisers are well-equipped to identify them and make sure that they are systematically and artfully solicited election after election. Our data show that almost 90% of those who made a contribution to a presidential candidate in 1988 were solicited to make a contribution to a presidential candidate in 1992.

It is not difficult to see why candidates focus much of their attention on attracting money from the same pool of motivated, regular contributors. Soliciting proven contributors is more cost effective than attempting to broaden the pool, for past contributors are more likely than noncontributors to give in the next election, and are generally easy to locate. Once a contributor appears on any presidential fundraising list, it is difficult not to appear again on some list in the future. All campaigns keep a careful record of those who give. At the end of the campaign, candidates can rent or sell their contributor lists, sometimes directly to presidential hopefuls in the next election cycle, and sometimes to professional list brokers who make them available to such candidates.[1] In addition to this, many solicitors who contact people in person are active in election after election, and they will go back to the same prospects year after year. Once you join the club of contributors, you will be asked repeatedly to remain a member.

The pool

Contributors of serious money are habitual presidential campaign givers. In 1988, 51% of our respondents reported that they gave to presidential candidates in most elections, and an additional 32% said that they gave in some elections. Only one in six made his or her first presidential contribution that year. These results are quite similar to those from the 1972 survey, when 57% of contributors reported that they gave to presidential candidates in most elections, and an additional 30% indicated that they had given in some elections – so the pool has been composed of habitual givers for some time.

In addition, not only are serious money contributors habitual donors, but many tend to be donors to multiple candidates. Fully half of all contributors gave to more than one presidential candidate in 1988, and nearly one in five gave to three or more.[2] The most common pattern of multiple giving was for contributors to losers also to give to winners in their own party. Substantial majorities of those who gave to Dole, du Pont, and Kemp also gave to Bush, and majorities of those who gave to Jackson and Simon also gave to Dukakis.[3] In addition, large minorities of those who gave to Babbitt, Gephardt, and Gore also gave to Dukakis. Approximately 7% of contributors gave to candidates of both parties in 1988, frequently to Bush or Dukakis. Overall, Bush received contributions from 39% of our sample, while Dukakis got money from 32% of all 1988 respondents. This pattern of multiple giving argues strongly against the proposition that contributors are principally mobilized by individual candidates on an ad hoc basis. It therefore seems, both from the pattern of habitual giving and the pattern of multiple giving, that those who contribute serious money constitute a large and fairly stable pool of presidential contributors.

Although all contributors are part of a pool of potential contributors, not all members of that pool give in every election. While more than half of our contributors indicated that they gave to presidential candidates "in most elections," it is unclear just what they meant by this phrase. Based on responses to survey questions that asked how frequently respondents have given in the past to Senate and House candidates and to parties, and whether they gave to them in 1988, we can estimate the meaning of phrases such as "in most elections" and "in some elections," and we can calculate what percentage of the presidential pool might be expected to contribute in any election cycle.[4] Overall, we expect that 67% of members of the contributing pool will contribute in any given election cycle. Our 1992 data show that 63% of the 1988 contributors did in fact give to a presidential candidate, a figure only four percentage points below our estimate.[5]

It is surprising that the percentage of 1988 contributors who gave in 1992 was so close to our estimate. The range of ideology represented by the candidates in both parties was far more narrow in 1992 than in 1988.[6] Indeed, those who gave to Robertson and especially to Jackson were the least likely to give again in 1992, for the political agendas of these candidates were not represented in the 1992 field.[7] In addition, among Democrats, most serious candidates started late, given Bush's popularity after the Gulf War, and it seemed early in the cycle that the reputedly "best" candidates had chosen not to run. Once the campaign began, most of the Democratic candidates, including Clinton, appeared to have had serious problems that might have precluded their eventual election. Among Republicans, there was initially a sense that Bush was the only game in town, and later there were serious questions about his ability to win in November.

For all of these reasons, it is surprising that the actual contribution rate in 1992 is only slightly below our estimate. Overall, the 1992 candidates did raise substantially less money than those who ran in 1988, raised it later in the cycle, and raised it with more effort. Our data suggest that this drop in total candidate receipts is not explained by lower contribution rates by serious money donors, but primarily by smaller contributions from those who gave. Among those who did give in 1992, half indicated that they gave substantially less money than they had in 1988. Thus it appears that many contributors respond to an unappealing set of candidates not by sitting out the campaign, but rather by making smaller contributions.

We asked those respondents from 1988 who made no contribution in 1992, or those who gave substantially less, to indicate the importance of various reasons for this change in their behavior. The most important reasons given for not contributing or for contributing less were that no candidate was well-qualified to be president and that no candidate represented the contributor's views. Substantial minorities of contributors also indicated that they did not give or gave less because they were disgusted with the nature of the campaign, they had less money to commit to political activities, and they saw little to be gained personally or professionally by contributing. Those who mentioned little or no professional or personal gain as a reason for not giving or for giving less were more likely to sit out the 1992 election altogether. This was especially true for individuals from the home state of a 1988 candidate, which suggests that they were initially attracted by the special material benefits that home-state candidates provide, and that none of the 1992 candidates could provide these same benefits.

Thus there exists a relatively stable pool of contributors, about a third of whom, for a variety of reasons, sit out a given election. A much smaller percentage may defect from the pool altogether. In every year there will also be an important number of first-time contributors, and these cumulatively have increased the size of the pool significantly since the mid-1970s. Thus the pool that constitutes the playing field upon which candidates compete for financial resources changes slowly from election to election.

Recruitment to the pool

Although campaigns generally concentrate on soliciting those who have given before, most candidates make some attempt to attract contributions from new prospects, and some campaigns make a major effort in this direction. Many citizens may be willing to send money to a presidential nomination candidate even if they have not done so before, and one task professional fundraisers face is to identify such citizens, pitch an attractive appeal to them, and thereby recruit them to the pool. Among contributors of serious money in 1988, 17% were first-time presidential contributors, compared to 13% in 1972.

There are many ways in which new members can be mobilized. Anecdotal evidence points to the effectiveness of historic media appeals to recruit first-time presidential contributors: Ronald Reagan's speech on behalf of Barry Goldwater in 1964, responses to which became the basis of many Republican and conservative mailing lists; John Anderson's 1980 full-page advertisement in the *New York Times*, which generated contributions from more than 7,500 contributors; and Jerry Brown's 800 number in 1992. We have no data to indicate to what extent these appeals mobilized first-time presidential contributors, but the presumption in fundraising circles is that the percentages were noteworthy in each case.

A second traditional recruiting ground is among contributors to candidates for other offices. Most presidential candidates solicit those who gave to them when they ran for lower office, whether or not they had ever given to a presidential candidate before. Some presidential candidates ask their major political supporters to make available their own list of contributors – or to send out appeals themselves on behalf of the candidate. For example, the Dukakis campaign made very effective use of several lists of contributors to friendly senators and members of Congress. Other campaigns seek to identify networks of regional or local party contributors. We report in Chapter 5 that Gephardt's campaign did this, focusing on Southern contributors who had never "played presidential" in past elections. Campaigns can often rent and prospect lists of contributors to non-presidential candidates and to parties. It is not surprising, therefore, to find in 1988 that 70% of those who were first-time presidential contributors had previously made a contribution to candidates for lower office or to parties, although about a third of these had made no more than one such contribution to each of these types of recipient.

A third way that fundraisers identify potential presidential contributors is to focus on those who contribute to political or social causes. This is done primarily by prospecting lists of interest group and PAC contributors. In 1988, 35% of those who were first-time presidential contributors had previously made a contribution to at least one PAC.

Fourth, fundraisers attempt to recruit from outside the political culture altogether, using a wide range of prospects, including commercial lists (such as owners of Volvos), charitable contribution lists, ZIP codes, magazine subscription lists, and the like. In selecting which lists to target, fundraisers begin with the assumption that the untapped who have a propensity to contribute will resemble in some demographic way those who have revealed their propensity by actually contributing.

Some candidates are more successful in recruiting new contributors than others. These include candidates with special ideological, geographic, ethnic, or other appeal. The most obvious example in 1988 was Pat Robertson, who sought to expand the contributing pool by adding newly mobilized charismatic Christians. Our data show that although 85% of his presidential contributors had given to his "700 Club" television show, fully a third had never before given to a presidential candidate, and 18% had never before made a political contribution of any kind. Although these data suggest that candidates such as Robertson with a widespread following outside of normal political channels can attract new money to the contributing pool, it is also striking that two-thirds of those who gave to Robertson had given before to a presidential candidate.

Although Dukakis attracted first-time contributors at a lower rate than Robertson (19% were making their first presidential contribution), he had many more total contributors of serious money than Robertson had and therefore recruited slightly more new members to the pool. Jackson's populist campaign might also have been expected to attract new contributors, especially among African American professionals. His mobilization efforts, however, seem to have occurred principally in his previous campaign for the presidency, for the data show that only 14% of his contributors were newly mobilized in 1988.

It appears that lists of newly mobilized contributors may be less valuable than lists of ongoing members of the pool. Although almost three in four of those who indicated that they give to presidential candidates "in most elections" gave again in 1992, less than half of those who made their first presidential gift in 1988 gave again four years later. Those newly mobilized into the contributor pool are the least likely to remain in it in the next election cycle. New members of the pool, however, are more likely to give again when a candidate appeals to the same set of motivations that attracted them in the first place. For example, a disproportionate number of Greek Orthodox contributors who had been mobilized in 1988 by Dukakis gave again, primarily to Paul Tsongas, in 1992.

Even though only 45% of those who gave to a presidential candidate for the first time in 1988 gave again in 1992, the quadrennial mobilization of new contributors is important because over the years they accumulate to a substantial portion of the pool and they can affect its composition. Because individuals who have been successfully solicited in the past constitute the core of future contributors, the ideological or other nature of the pool of contributors may be altered by the successful mobilization efforts of one candidate in a given year. Thus the cumulative results of the mobilization efforts of a succession of candidates may have a profound effect on the fundraising potential of future candidates.

Financial participation by the contributing pool: Giving to other political actors

The pool of contributors of serious money to presidential nomination candidates is part of a larger pool of political contributors, and few presidential nomination contributors confine their giving to candidates for the presidency. This is true for two reasons. First, the factors that motivate a gift to a presidential candidate in many cases will motivate contributions to governors, senators, par-

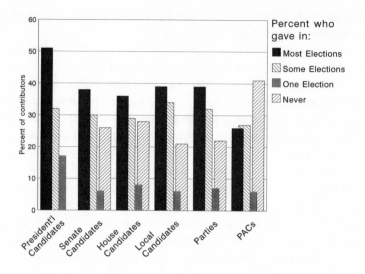

Figure 3.1. Frequency of giving at all levels in 1988.

ties, and PACs. Second, new entrants to the pool are typically recruited from those who give to other types of political campaigns. The data in Figure 3.1 show that many presidential contributors give frequently to candidates at all levels of government, to political parties, and to PACs. Indeed, nearly four in ten give in "most" elections to Senate candidates. The same is true for House candidates, local candidates, and/or parties, and more than a quarter give in most elections to a PAC. These percentages are nearly identical to those from the 1972 survey, pointing to the overall structural stability of the pool.

Contributor estimates of their own frequency of giving are borne out by their patterns of actual contributions in 1988. Approximately half of the presidential contributing pool gave to Senate candidates in 1988; the same is true for House candidates and for parties. These percentages are impressive, especially in light of the fact that 20% of the respondents lived in states with no Senate race, and many respondents lived in congressional districts where there was either an uncontested or only a nominally contested House election. Fully 21% gave to Senate candidates outside their own states. Furthermore, 20% reported giving to more than one House candidate, more than a quarter gave to a House candidate outside their district, and 15% gave to a House candidate outside their state.

Since we asked presidential contributors simply if they gave to House and Senate candidates and to parties (and not how much they gave), their responses do not enable us to tell what percentages gave *serious money* in most elections. An analysis of the lists of FEC contributors helps shed some light on this question, and also supports the proposition that large percentages of presidential contributors are persistent givers to candidates at other levels of government, even in off-year elections.[8] Based on this analysis, we estimate that *at least* 36% gave serious money in 1990 to Senate candidates; the same is true for House candidates and for party committees.

We can classify contributors of serious money into four groups, based on their patterns of giving to candidates and party committees. This creates a scale that we refer to later in the book as the Index of Campaign Giving. In the top category are the 20% of contributors who reported that they give in most elections to *all* of the following: candidates for president, Senate or House, local office, and parties. In the second category are an additional 44% of contributors who give in most elections to one or more of these types of candidates or to parties but who do not give in most elections to all of them. Third, 26% of the contributors do not give in *most* elections to any type of candidate or to parties, but they do give in *some* elections to at least one type of candidate or to a party. Finally, 9% of the contributors have given no more than once to any type of candidate or to parties. The distribution of contributors between these four types in 1988 is nearly identical to the distribution for 1972, again pointing to the pool's structural stability over time. We will use this summary measure of the extent and level of contributing activity in this and subsequent chapters.

Giving to candidates and parties is, of course, only one dimension of contributing behavior, and the activity of individuals in this area is related to their activities on other dimensions. For example, giving to PACs is strongly related to giving to candidates and parties. Our Index of Campaign Giving is correlated with frequency of PAC giving at .39. Fully 64% of those who score highest on our Index of Campaign Giving contribute to PACs in most elections, but an additional 20% have never given to PACs. This confirms the findings of Jones and Miller (1985) that PAC and campaign giving are distinct but correlated activities. Thus the pool of presidential contributors may be viewed as a subset of a much larger population of contributors to a variety of candidates, political parties, and PACs.

Other campaign participation

It is sometimes argued that the rise of direct mail fundraising has nurtured a group of "checkbook citizens" who contribute money to politics but do not participate in other ways. The argument implies a normative judgment that campaign participation is a more complete form of participation, and that contributions from isolated citizens do not build bonds of political community. Most contributors of serious money to presidential nomination candidates, however, even those newly recruited to the pool, are typically much more politically active than average citizens. Of course, recruitment to the contributor pool may serve as an avenue to further political involvement for individuals who had previously been politically inactive. In this circumstance, contributing is a form of participation that may lead to other types of political involvement.

Our data confirm that some contributors of serious money to presidential candidates do not otherwise participate in *campaign* activity, and that contributors in 1988 were less active in this respect than those in 1972. In 1988, for example, only 14% of our contributors reported *working* for presidential candidates in most elections, a figure markedly lower than the 51% who reported *contributing* in most elections. A noticeably larger 24% of those who gave to a presidential candidate in 1972 reported working for presidential candidates in most elections.

We created a typology of participation in a fashion identical to the one for contribution behavior discussed above. This produces a scale that we refer to as the Index of Campaign Work. In the top category are the 7% of contributors who reported that they work in most elections for *all* of the following: candidates for president, Senate or House, local office, and parties. In the second category are an additional 17% of contributors who work in most elections for one or more of these types of candidates or for parties but who do not work in most elections for all of them. Third, 38% of the contributors do not work in most elections for any type of candidate or for parties but do work in some elections for at least one type of candidate or for a party. Finally, 45% of the contributors have worked no more than once for any type of candidate or for parties.

Although there was a decline in campaign activity from 1972 to 1988,[9] the 1988 data on campaign activity do not by themselves suggest that there is a large number of "checkbook" participants. Individuals who work in campaigns almost inevitably do so more selectively than they give, and the small percentage of individuals who do work in most elections at all levels are likely to have politics as their primary profession or avocation. These levels of working, though more modest than those of giving, actually represent considerable political participation.

Furthermore, contributors engage in a wide range of other political activities. About a third of the contributors in 1988 said they had held a party position, a public elective office, or a public appointive office. Nearly eight out of ten indicated that they had on occasion tried to influence an act of Congress. Almost 60% said they had written to a House member, a Senator, or the president; more than a third reported having spoken directly with a member of Congress, senator, or president, or with a member of their staffs, or said they had worked through informal or formal groups or parties. About 13% said they had taken part in a demonstration or other visible means of protest in order to influence an act of Congress.

In 1972, noticeably larger percentages of contributors wrote, spoke, and demonstrated; somewhat larger percentages worked through informal groups. For example, 22% of contributors in 1972 had demonstrated, compared to 13% in 1988; 78% of 1972 contributors wrote to policy makers compared to 59% in 1988; 52% in 1972 had spoken with a policy maker, compared to 36% in 1988. These larger percentages may well have been the product of the political circumstances of the 1960s and early 1970s, especially the civil rights movement and Vietnam. There was no substantial decline, and perhaps a real net gain, between 1972 and 1988 in working through formal groups, including parties.[10]

These data show that the contributing pool is composed of individuals who regularly give to candidates and party committees, who regularly contact government officials, and who occasionally work in campaigns. Although some contributors may be characterized as "checkbook citizens," most are involved in a wide range of political activities.

Partisanship

Contributors are more likely than the mass public to be strong partisans, and so the contributing pool is loosely divided along party lines. Nearly half the contributors say they give exclusively to candidates from one party. An additional 46% say they give *predominately* to candidates from one party. Only 6% say they give equally to candidates in both parties; most of these consider themselves to be independents or independents leaning toward one or the other party. Only 7% gave to candidates in both parties in 1988, and 13% gave to a candidate in the party opposite the one with which the contributor identified. The percentages were almost identical for these same contributors in 1992.

These percentages are surprisingly low, given the level of cross-party solicitation. Of the 1988 contributors who were solicited again in 1992, 39% received at least one targeted solicitation from a candidate in the opposite party, although seven-eighths were solicited by candidates within their own party.[11] The strength of partisanship is well illustrated by the fact that so few of those solicited by candidates from the other party actually give across party lines.

Giving across party lines was far more common among Republicans than among Democrats. More than one in six of Republican contributors gave to a Democratic candidate. These cross-party contributors are discussed in more detail in Chapter 5.

Demographic characteristics

We have established that all candidates in 1988 raised a substantial majority of their serious money from the existing pool of contributors. Candidates must therefore consider to some extent the demographic characteristics of the members of this pool in making their decisions about whom to target and how to approach them. To understand the decisions made by campaigns, it is therefore important to profile these demographic characteristics. The demographic characteristics of the pool have important normative implications as well. Since contributors are influential actors in the selection of presidential candidates, and campaign considerations are never far from the mind of a sitting president, it is important to know how those who give to presidential candidates differ from the rest of the public. These normative issues are most obvious in the comparison of the affluence of contributors with ordinary citizens, but other demographic differences may be important as well.

Our data allow us to compare the demographic characteristics of contributors in the 1972 pool to those in the 1988 pool, and to compare the latter to respondents in the 1988 National Election Study (NES) who indicated that they contributed money to candidates. In Table 3.1 we show the demographic profiles of each group. Comparisons between 1972 and 1988 must be made cautiously, since some contributors in 1972 gave early to avoid the disclosure regulations that went into effect during that campaign and are not included in the sample. In addition, the NES item asked respondents whether they had given to political candidates. Those who answered "yes" may differ from our respondents in at least two ways. First, they may not have given to a presidential candidate and instead contributed to candidates for Congress or for state or local office. Second, they may have given small gifts that did not aggregate to more than $200. Approximately 6% of NES respondents indicated that they had given to a political candidate.

The campaign finance reforms enacted after the 1972 election were designed in part to expand the size of the contributing pool, and also to

Table 3.1. *Demographic characteristics of contributors*

	Contributor samples, %		NES, %	
	1972	1988	Gave 1988	Didn't Give
High school or less	10	6	24	58
Some college	15	15	32	23
College	21	22	23	11
Some graduate, graduate degree	54	57	22	9
Under $50,000	54	18	62	85
$50,000-$99,000	18	21	38	15
$100,000-$249,999	28	30	na	na
$250,000 and up		30	na	na
Female	24	27	52	57
Male	76	73	48	43
White	na	96	86	86
Black	na	2	12	12

na = item not in survey.

broaden its demographic composition. The data in Table 3.1, however, show that the contributors in our 1972 and 1988 surveys are surprisingly similar. The pool of contributors in both 1972 and 1988 was predominantly well-educated, affluent, white, and male. More than half the respondents in each year had education beyond a college degree; nearly 30% in 1988 held an M.D., Ph.D., LLB, or its equivalent.

An impressive 28% of 1972 contributors had family incomes above $100,000, and 30% of the 1988 contributors had incomes in excess of $250,000 – a figure roughly equal to the $100,000 category in 1972 after adjustment for inflation. Although these comparisons must be made with caution, we find no evidence that either the education or income level of serious money contributors changed substantially in real terms between 1972 and 1988.[12] It seems reasonable to conclude, therefore, that although the reforms encouraged many more people to enter the process, these people were demographically very similar to those who were active before the FECA.

The high level of socioeconomic achievement among contributors of serious money is not surprising, but it is important to note that socioeconomic achievement is not limited to contributors to centrist party candidates such as Bush, Dole, Gore, and Dukakis. Although both Robertson and Jackson attracted less-educated and less-affluent contributors, their donors were also generally well-educated and affluent compared to the general public. Nearly all of Jackson's contributors and 84% of those who gave to Robertson had at least some college education, and both candidates had more contributors with family incomes in excess of $100,000 than with incomes below $25,000.[13]

The contributors identified in the NES had predictably lower levels of education and income but were nonetheless better-educated and more affluent than noncontributors. The difference between the NES results and those of our survey may be due to differences in the size of contributions, for many of those identified in the NES doubtlessly made small contributions. In our survey, those whom we sampled as making a small contribution were noticeably less affluent and less educated than those who made larger gifts.[14] Fewer than 1% of contributors with incomes of under $25,000 gave a gift of $1,000, compared with nearly half of those with incomes of $250,000 or more. In contrast, nearly half of those sampled with incomes of less than $25,000 made a contribution of $50 or less, compared with less than 1% of those with incomes over $250,000.

The contributor pool was overwhelmingly male in both 1972 and 1988. Approximately three out of four contributors in both surveys were men. This is somewhat surprising in light of the focused efforts by both parties to expand participation by women. The underrepresentation of women among serious money donors may be a function of two factors. First, campaign finance professionals told us that women are more likely to contribute to causes such as PACs and interest groups, and to state and local candidates, while men are more likely to give to candidates for national office. Second, women generally make smaller donations, even after income differences are controlled.[15] It is likely that these gender differences will begin to erode in future elections. In 1992, PACs that specialized in raising money from women mobilized large sums on behalf of women candidates for Congress, and many of these PAC contributors also gave directly to women candidates (Nelson 1994; Rimmerman 1994). There was a much smaller male advantage among those contributors identified by the NES.

The contributors in our surveys also were overwhelmingly and disproportionately white. This was true despite the candidacy of Jackson. The NES data show that equal proportions of blacks and whites made contributions, suggesting the possibility that Jackson and other black candidates attracted large numbers of small contributions from the African American community that did not aggregate to more than $200. Anecdotal evidence indicates that Jackson frequently collected large numbers of small contributions during his many visits to African American churches in 1984 and 1988 (Hertzke 1993, p.123). Nearly 60% of the small numbers of blacks who responded to our

1988 survey gave to Jackson, but more than two-thirds of those who gave serious money to Jackson were white. Among contributors of serious money, Jackson certainly achieved a "rainbow" coalition.

The demographic makeup of the pool of serious money contributors has changed little if at all between 1972 and 1988, despite the reforms enacted after the 1972 election. There are three possible reasons for this lack of change. First, the financial resources needed for membership in the pool guarantee that members will always be affluent. The size of the reporting cutoff has roughly kept pace with inflation, and the pool was about as affluent in 1988 as in 1972. This level of affluence is most common among well-educated white men, and this explains the demographic continuity on these traits as well.

Second, although the reforms provided incentives to gather contributions from many more individuals, we have seen above that it is more efficient for campaigns to target people who are similar to those who already give to presidential candidates, and especially those who give serious money to candidates for other political offices. These individuals are the most likely to make the same calculation concerning the costs and benefits of contributing as those who had given previously. The reforms therefore may have expanded the number of contributors, but only by adding additional members who were very similar to those already in the pool.

Third, those who solicit others personally to make a contribution usually come from the existing pool of contributors, and may be expected to solicit friends and associates who are similar to themselves in socioeconomic characteristics. Hence, though the pool has expanded, there are reasons to help explain why its overall profile has not changed.

There are noticeable differences in the demographic profiles of contributors to candidates in each party, and to different candidates within the parties. These data are shown in Table 3.2. Democratic contributors exhibited higher levels of education, and Republican contributors showed higher incomes. The educational differences are striking: 58% of those who gave to Democratic candidates held an advanced degree, compared with 35% of those who gave to Republicans. In contrast, 37% of those who gave to Republican candidates had incomes of over $250,000, compared to 23% of those who gave to Democrats. These income differences are even larger when the newly mobilized Robertson contributors are excluded from the analysis. When these new pool entrants are left out, more than 43% of those sampled as contributing to Republican candidates had incomes of $250,000 or more. This reflects a different underlying economic base for each party, with Republicans attracting money from wealthy

Table 3.2. *Demographic characteristics of contributors by candidate: 1988 (%)*

	Bush	Dole	du Pont	Kemp	Robertson
Education					
< College	17	9	30	23	51
> College	46	65	46	54	30
Income					
< $100,000	9	13	10	19	54
> $250,000	47	54	40	36	4
Female	26	13	20	20	38
White	98	99	100	99	98
South	34	18	6	16	46
Mean age	55	54	56	54	51
Denomination					
Mainline Prot.	55	42	58	39	20
Evangel. Prot.	0	3	2	10	51
Catholic	20	24	14	26	4
Jewish	7	17	4	5	0
No affiliation	6	6	3	11	1

businesspeople with college degrees and Democrats receiving contributions from somewhat less affluent professionals who hold advanced degrees.

Other broad party differences are evident in these data. For example, Democrats are more likely than Republicans to attract donations from women and from Jewish contributors, patterns that both fit data on voting differences (Bendyna and Lake 1994; Cook 1994; Sigelman 1993).

Within each party, different candidates attract different types of contributors. Among Republicans, the most obvious distinction is between those who gave to Robertson and those who gave to other Republicans. Robertson's contributors were noticeably less educated and affluent; more were Southern, more were female, and more were predominantly from evangelical churches. Additional analysis suggests that more than two-thirds reported a "charismatic" experience, suggesting that Robertson mobilized only a relatively narrow base of evangelical Christians (Wilcox 1992).

Among Democrats, those who gave to Jesse Jackson are markedly less educated and affluent. Also, Jackson's donors include higher percentages of blacks and women than do contributors to other Democratic candidates. Gephardt and especially Gore attracted Southern money. Simon attracted the oldest contributors – there is a decade of difference between the mean age of

	Babbitt	Dukakis	Gephardt	Gore	Jackson	Simon
Education						
< College	9	13	31	12	34	14
> College	77	77	55	63	47	65
Income						
< $100,000	14	12	11	10	40	27
> $250,000	25	26	18	24	6	19
Female	32	30	28	28	49	32
White	100	97	92	100	63	97
South	12	4	54	69	9	13
Mean age	48	50	51	47	54	58
Denomination						
Mainline Prot.	30	21	47	46	22	38
Evangel. Prot.	2	0	10	16	21	2
Catholic	20	13	14	11	9	15
Jewish	22	33	10	18	11	18
No affiliation	17	5	8	3	16	16

his contributors and those to Babbitt and Gore. Dukakis had special appeal to Jewish donors.

In Chapter 5 we focus more fully on the resources that enable candidates to attract different types of contributors. Although this group is distinctive when compared to the general public, it is important to recognize that the contributor pool is not homogeneous. Instead, it is composed of clusters of contributors who can be mobilized by different candidates using different types of appeals with varying degrees of success. In some elections, no candidate will appeal to a particular base of financial support, while in others that base will be cross-pressured between two attractive candidates. There remains, however, the strong assumption that contributors from any segment, once mobilized, will be responsive to an appropriate future appeal. The effectiveness of such appeals depends in part upon the political motives of the contributors in the pool.

Motivations of contributors

As campaigns identify the segment of the pool that will comprise their financial constituency, it is necessary for them to consider the motivations of those

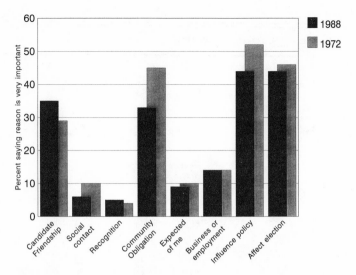

Figure 3.2. Reasons for contributing: 1972 and 1988.

whom they wish to attract. We asked the contributors both in 1972 and in 1988 to indicate the importance to them of a variety of reasons for participating in politics. The exact wording of the items can be found in Appendix II. Figure 3.2 shows the percentage of respondents saying that each reason was very important for each year.

In both 1972 and 1988, the most frequently cited reasons for political involvement were to make a difference in the outcome of an election and to influence the policies of government. Many respondents also indicated a personal friendship with the candidate, although it is not clear from these data what exact type of relationship this indicates.[16] Others stated they were active in politics out of a sense of community obligation. Fewer admitted to a business motive or that they were active in politics because it was expected of someone in their position.[17] Only a small minority of respondents indicated that their political activity was motivated by a desire for recognition or for social contacts.

The largest change from 1972 to 1988 was a decline in the importance of a sense of community obligation as a factor for contributing. There was a smaller decline between 1972 and 1988 in the proportion of respondents who cited influencing policy as a very important motive. In contrast, there was a modest increase in the importance of friendship for a candidate. These changes may reflect differences in the two elections: campaigns generally are more candidate-centered today, and the 1972 election was dominated by a strong policy concern over the Vietnam war. The changes may also reflect the different mix of candidates; in 1972 the Democratic nomination was won by an ideological candidate whose supporters wanted to influence government policy, while in 1988 the Democratic nomination was won by a technocrat who wanted competently to manage government.

Wilson (1973) described three distinct motives for participation in social organizations – a desire for policy outcomes or purposive benefits, a desire for social or solidary benefits, and a desire for material benefits. Our factor analysis of the reasons described above confirmed that these three sets of motives exist for political contributors as well. The items "influence policies of government" and "make a difference in the outcome of an election" exemplify and have very high loadings on a "purposive" factor. "Feeling of recognition" and "enjoy the social contacts" load highly on a "solidary" factor. "Business and employment reasons" and "expected of someone in my position" load highly on a "material" factor. These last two reasons may also reflect the contributor's relationship with a solicitor as well as with the candidate. The factor structures in 1972 and 1988 were remarkably similar. The three factor scores will be used as measures of the importance of purposive, solidary, and material motives to the respondent. The higher the score on a factor, the more important that motive is to the respondent. A positive factor score is above average in comparison to other respondents; a negative factor score is below average.

These motives shape the calculations that the political participants make in weighing the costs and benefits of contributing and are thus key to understanding their decisions to work for and contribute to campaigns. Thus we expect to find that the more important each motive is to the respondent, the more likely she or he is to give to and to work in campaigns. The relationship between the motives and the indices of working and giving in campaigns is shown in Figure 3.3. The figure shows the mean scores of motivations for each category of campaign giving and working. Here, we look at those who had given in at least one presidential election before 1988; thus there are no respondents in the first category of the Index of Campaign Giving. We have defined the precise meaning of each category above. The first category represents the least activity and the fourth the highest.

The figure supports our expectations and reveals some differences in the magnitude of the relationships. Correlations between our measures of these motives and the Index of Campaign Giving for those who are not first-time presidential contributors are all significant and approximately equal in magni-

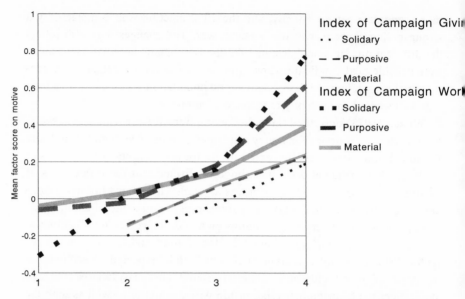

Figure 3.3. Motives and campaign contributing and working. *Note:* Scores on Index of Campaign Work: 4–work in most elections for presidential, congressional, and local candidates and parties; 3–work in most elections for one or more, but not all, of the preceding list; 2–work in some elections for one or more of the above list, but not in most elections to any; 1–work in not more than one election for any in the above list. Scores on Index of Campaign Giving are similarly defined with category 1 omitted.

tude: all three motives lead independently to campaign contributions. The correlations with our Index of Campaign Work show a markedly different pattern, however. Solidary motives are by far the strongest predictor of campaign work, although the other two motives are also statistically significant. This result makes good sense, for those who work on campaigns are more likely to value the social interactions that these activities provide. Purposive motives show the second strongest relationship, which indicates that people who care about causes are willing to donate their time as well as their money.

Conclusions

Campaigns appeal primarily to an established pool of those who often give to presidential campaigns. Although some members of the pool sit out some presidential elections, many give in most and some, perhaps, give in all. These regular donors are relatively easy to identify, and therefore to solicit. Moreover, campaigns are more likely to receive money from these proven contributors than from those prospects solicitors attempt to add to the pool.

Of course, some candidates can expand the pool by bringing in new participants. In 1972 and 1988, around one in eight contributors to most candidates were new to presidential giving, but fully a third of Robertson's contributors were newly mobilized. New entrants to the pool are less likely than past contributors to remain in the pool for the next election cycle, although our data do not allow us to determine whether they return in future elections. Yet the pool does grow incrementally by the recruitment efforts of campaigns, and we see in Chapter 6 that most new 1988 contributors were solicited again in 1992.

Those who give money to presidential campaigns are generally white, male, well-educated, affluent, and active in contributing at several levels of government. They are less active in working for campaigns, but they are far more active than the average citizen. Although the pool appears distinctively different from the general public, it is less internally homogeneous than it first might appear. Not only are there partisan differences, but there are demographic and motivational differences that can result in significant compositional differences in candidate coalitions.

Contributors are active in politics in order to seek different types of benefits. Some seek material benefits for their firms or their families, others enjoy the solidary benefits of socializing, often with those who share their partisanship. Others are motivated by purposive benefits and try to elect candidates who share their ideological views. To attract money from contributors with differing motives, campaigns have evolved special techniques. The next chapter discusses the personal networks that mobilize those with material and solidary motives, and the impersonal solicitations that tap into purposive motivations.

4. Mobilizing the pool: Methods of soliciting campaign funds

The pool of serious money contributors is a resource to be mobilized, not a force that presses itself on presidential hopefuls. People do not give to candidates spontaneously, but because they are asked to give. Successful candidates must therefore develop strategies to determine who has the greatest potential to contribute money to the campaign, and how to tap such people.

Campaigns make decisions about how to try to collect money by estimating how to get the greatest return for the least commitment of resources (e.g., money, candidate time, staff time). Ultimately the composition of each candidate's financial constituency is a function of the candidate's resources and the campaign's decisions about how to take advantage of them. These decisions result in the specific choices of whom to approach and how to approach them.

There are two basic methods of raising money in presidential campaigns. Candidates can hire direct mail or telemarketing firms to solicit citizens whose names appear on various lists. Candidates can also attempt to build networks of solicitors who ask their friends and business associates to contribute money. Many candidates use both approaches, but in 1988 each candidate used one of these techniques far more than the other.

There are differences among candidates in the optimal ways to raise money because potential contributors respond to different candidate characteristics in deciding whether or not to make a contribution. Successful impersonal solicitations are likely to involve strong emotional appeals by candidates who represent the ideological wings of their party. In contrast, individuals who give in response to solicitations from a fundraiser whom they know personally may be less interested in the issue positions and qualities of the candidate to whom they are contributing than they are in the cultivation of a relationship with the individual who asked them to give. Candidates tied closely to party networks and officeholders who have access to the policy agenda are especially able to offer solicitors the rewards they seek for participation.

As described in Chapter 3, all potential contributors must weigh the opportunity costs of making a contribution against an array of purposive, solidary, or material benefits that such a contribution might produce. Individuals differ in the importance they assign to these three types of benefits. For some, issues are paramount and they choose among candidates based on proximity to a candidate on one or more policy positions. Others seek the social benefits that arise in the course of interacting with other contributors and political actors. In addition some may contribute to further their own careers in politics. Finally, some contributors seek to profit financially. They may establish business contacts with other contributors, create obligations from those who solicited them, repay obligations, or open the way to receive direct benefits from government, including contracts and targeted legislation of benefit to themselves.

Some contributors are motivated by a single objective, while others are motivated by a mixture of goals. Fundraisers are aware of the many goals that exist among members of the contributing pool. The primary methods of solicitation have evolved as a result of experiments among competing fundraising professionals trying to raise the most money for the least expenditure of resources. Changes in both campaign finance laws and technology have shaped the course of this evolution.

Thus the composition of each candidate's financial constituency is a function of the nature of the candidate's resources, including those that enable the candidate to offer purposive, solidary, or material benefits. It is also a function of the campaign's decisions about what methods to use to exploit those resources. The composition of the candidate's financial constituency – those who make contributions to the campaign – in turn, has an impact on the conduct of the campaign, and perhaps on the nature of the presidency that may ensue.

Most simply, if the contributors to a campaign are not numerous enough or generous enough, the candidate is unlikely to have the resources to win election. Contributors and solicitors who are not strongly committed to a candidate may disappear if the candidacy falters and the prospects for election diminish. Strongly committed contributors can support a candidate through difficult times and sustain the possibility of a comeback. Further, key fundraisers or groups of contributors may reap the rewards of election and have influence in a successful candidate's administration. Ambassadorships are a traditional plum, but key finance officials have, on occasion, held central policy positions as well.

Raising money through direct mail and telemarketing

The mechanics of direct mail are straightforward. Most candidates start with a "house list" of those who have contributed to them before, typically to campaigns for lower office or to their campaign PACs. In 1988, for example, Dole and Kemp began with house lists from these two sources; Bush used a large list of political acquaintances developed over many years, as well as a candidate PAC; du Pont created a house list based on family connections, which was referred to in the trade as his "Christmas card" list; and Robertson started with the list of people who had signed a petition urging him to run. Most of these were also regular donors to his "700 Club" television show, and had given repeatedly to his religious solicitations.

While they are milking the house list, candidates also try to broaden their donor base by prospecting other lists. They mail to a test sample from proven lists, such as National Rifle Association (NRA) members, National Wildlife Federation donors, National Abortion Rights Action League (NARAL) supporters, *New Republic* subscribers, or contributors to friendly political figures who make their lists available. Such lists are generally rented, and candidates may "keep" a name and add it to their house list if the person contributes to the campaign.[1] To increase the potential yield, prospect lists can be cross-checked against other lists to narrow the demographics and politics of those solicited.[2] Such cross-checking to refine a prospect list is not yet the norm for presidential campaigns, but it is becoming more common.

If the prospecting test proves to be successful, then the entire list will be rented and used. Success is determined by the long-term potential for the list, not the immediate return. A list producing 35 cents on the dollar may be marginally "successful" for two reasons. First, since the small gifts typically made in response to a direct mail solicitation are fully matched, the returns will effectively be doubled. For example, Scott McKenzie, a direct mail fundraiser for Kemp and Buchanan, noted that Kemp lost money in his initial prospecting – between $800,000 and $900,000 in one mailing – but made a small profit because of the match. Second, those who respond will be resolicited repeatedly, and most campaigns, on average, will succeed over time in doubling the initial contribution. A large percentage of these subsequent contributions will be fully matched also, so a campaign may project, with the match, a long-term yield between three and four times the initial return. It is in this way that direct mail contributors are often induced to give enough to reach the "serious money" level.[3] Furthermore, follow-up mailings produce a much higher yield and are therefore much less costly per dollar raised. Hence resolicitation is central to the calculus of direct mail.

This whole process, however, remains expensive. The perpetual prospecting needed to build a large donor base consumes huge quantities of cash. Since time is of the essence, campaigns typically recommit large percentages of initial receipts to subsequent mailings in a double-or-nothing kind of strategy, and although statistical projections limit the risk, they do not eliminate it entirely, since political climates can change rapidly and render prior projections inaccurate. For example, the stock market fell sharply during one Kemp mailing that praised the Reagan economic program, and the response rate fell with it.[4]

For all these reasons, it is not surprising to find that many direct mail campaigns (such as those for Philip Crane in 1980 and Pat Robertson in 1988) expended very large percentages of the money received on the process of raising the money itself. Most professionals believe that direct mail is more costly per dollar raised than personal-acquaintance networking, where the contributions are typically larger and a lot of the costs are absorbed by the fundraisers.

Successful direct mail fundraising relies on both the medium and the message. Most practitioners agree that such variables as the appearance of the envelope, the class of postage, and the length of the letter (the longer the better) are important. Yet Buchanan mailed several solicitations that violated normal industry practice and did so productively. McKenzie told us that Buchanan had more success with Kemp's house list from 1988 than Kemp had had; he successfully used religion-based lists, which are usually losing propositions for political candidates; and he did better than Bush with mail solicitation. His successes suggest that sometimes the type of package may be less important than the message, the messenger, and the electoral climate.

Direct mail works best for candidates who can make an appeal to voters on the basis of "values," typically the ideological messages of left and right, although centrist candidates like Anderson in 1980 and Hart in 1984 mounted successful direct mail efforts that resonated with people's basic values. The professionals agree that those who send money in response to a direct mail solicitation are principally motivated by anger, outrage, frustration, or, more positively, by intense compassion, inspiration, or a strong vision of the future.

It should be noted that moderate candidates can also raise a limited amount of money through the mail from specially targeted lists. For example, in 1988 Bush and Dole raised modest amounts by mailing to those who had given to their candidate PACs. In 1992, Bush, an incumbent president, raised between $4 and $5 million by mailing to his "house list" of those who had attended his fundraising dinners in 1988. But in this case many of those who were solicited by mail needed a personal phone call (sometimes two or three) before they contributed – so this cannot really count as a successful centrist "direct mail" effort.

Dukakis also raised money by mail in 1988, but the limited extent of his success may serve to illustrate the typical experience of a centrist candidate. He mailed approximately 800,000 pieces during the course of the campaign to the house list he had developed during his years as governor, and he received about 28,000 returns averaging $65 per return, for a response rate of 3.4%. The mailings generated $1,800,000 before the match and $2,900,000 after, netting about $1,400,000 – an impressive result, but still only about 10% of the gross he raised from all sources and a smaller percentage of his total net.

Dukakis also prospected by renting samples of commercially available lists and by obtaining house lists of political supporters, especially from Congress. In this endeavor, he was much less successful. The prospecting campaign mailed 1.3 million pieces and received only 15,000 responses averaging $32 per response, for a response rate of about 1%.[5] He grossed just under $500,000 from these mailings, netting less than $100,000 before the match, but receiving more than $400,000 in matching funds. (This provides another dramatic illustration of how the match can make an otherwise unprofitable or marginally profitable list worthwhile.) Even with the match, this large prospecting effort produced total revenues of less than 4% of his gross from all sources and an even smaller percentage of his total net. Faced with these disappointing results, the Dukakis campaign assigned its scarce fundraising resources to a more promising method of solicitation.

Resolicitation efforts may employ media and messages different from those used for the initial solicitations. For example, telemarketing may be used as a follow-through to a successful direct mail solicitation: many campaigns phone those who responded to their direct mail appeals, thank them for the contribution, and ask for more, often citing some immediate or pressing need for cash, such as a crucial upcoming primary. And in resolicitation efforts, professionals often try not only to preserve the value-laden message of the initial solicitation but also to activate a social motive for giving. This can be done by encouraging contributors to feel that they are part of a group effort, a "family" of contributors, as one fundraiser styles it. Follow-up appeals may therefore include: special "insider" information about the campaign; quotations from other contributors to exemplify the familial nature of the contributing cohort, and language recognizing the importance to the candidate of the contributor's financial sacrifice.

As our results indicate, direct mail campaigns for presidential nomination candidates tend to succeed more among older people than among younger ones, despite the fact that some types of organizations and some types of candidates (especially women candidates at the state and local levels) are doing well with mailings to younger age cohorts. Some campaign professionals argue that this is a generational phenomenon. They suggest that the generation that came of age during the Great Depression is more print-oriented than subsequent television-influenced generations, and is more likely to respond to partisan mailings, given its political socialization in the 1930s and before. It may also be somewhat less technologically sophisticated than younger generations, and so more readily impressed by a seemingly personal letter apparently signed by a candidate. If this hypothesis is correct, then the generation of those who respond to direct mail is cycling out of the electorate, and the political role of direct mail will diminish substantially.

Other fundraisers argue that the propensity to respond to direct mail is a life-cycle phenomenon, and that older people enjoy getting and reading mail, have more time to absorb the message, and have more disposable income to give to candidates. If this is true, there will be a golden age for direct mail in the future when the baby boomer generation, with its inherited assets, bulges the percentage of those over age 60.

Although mail still dominates impersonal fundraising methods, candidates have begun to use telemarketing more in recent years, in part to deal with these age-based limits of direct mail. Whether telemarketing is more effective among a non-print-oriented cohort, or whether it is more able to penetrate the consciousness of busy individuals who routinely throw away anything that looks like a mail solicitation, it is perceived by some fundraisers as an alternative to direct mail.

Telemarketing can be done by campaign volunteers or by firms that establish phone banks to call prospective donors and ask for gifts. Calls can be made locally or by use of WATS lines, nationally. The size of the telemarketing operation can vary from a handful of people making highly targeted calls to a large broad-based operation with huge banks of telephones. As is the case with direct mail, the federal match augments the reach of telemarketing operations by making them more cost effective.

Telemarketing has advantages in addition to its ability to reach those who toss solicitation letters in the trash. First, according to campaign finance specialist Michael MacLeod, the telemarketing solicitor can negotiate with the prospective donor over the dollar amount she or he will give. Some fundraising specialists believe that professionally made telemarketing calls, properly spaced in time, will produce larger total dollar amounts than will a sequence of mailings to the same person. Also, telemarketing provides a lot more flexibility in presenting what professionals call the "case-statement" – the campaign's message. Not only can a telemarketing campaign change its message in response to events much more quickly than can a direct mail campaign, but a well-trained telephone solicitor can get some immediate feedback from the potential donor in the course of the conversation and can therefore to some extent tailor the pitch during the call.

Moreover, telemarketing campaigns sometimes gather information about the person called that can be stored and used to advantage in making subsequent appeals. This practice is especially useful with donors of large amounts. In addition, telemarketing can be used to project a political message in the course of the fundraising appeal that has an impact on follow-through mail solicitation efforts. Some telemarketing campaigns have produced a "halo effect" that augmented subsequent direct mail efforts by 10% or more. Also, campaign finance specialists say there is a subset of the contributing population that genuinely likes phone calls and responds much more positively to them than to mail – even when they are willing to read the mail. Specialists claim that some are so enthusiastic that telemarketing solicitors have trouble getting them off the phone, thereby seriously diminishing the efficiency of the operation. Finally, sophisticated telemarketing can be used to personalize the pitch in less artificial ways than direct mail can – and this can produce a better yield, since people generally appreciate a high degree of personalization.

The main drawback of telemarketing is cost. Although under some circumstances it can require less money up front than direct mail, it is usually much more expensive. Professionally done, costs can range from a few dollars up to fifteen dollars a call, depending on the training of the solicitor, the length of the message, and the degree to which calls are made outside of a local calling area. Furthermore, since few people will give their credit card numbers over the phone, telemarketing requires a follow-up mailing to collect the money. This adds to the cost. For these reasons, professional telemarketing is not used frequently in prospecting political lists – which is why we found that only 3% of serious money contributors were first approached through telemarketing. It is used much more often in follow-through solicitation after a prospect has already made a contribution, or in cultivating a house list.

Campaigns can dramatically reduce the cost of telemarketing through the use of volunteers making local phone calls, and therefore some operations based on volunteer personnel can engage in list prospecting. The problem is that many of the advantages of telemarketing cannot be fully realized with untrained volunteer personnel making the calls.

Many experts assert that telemarketing has a promising future, and most agree that its use in political campaigns is expanding steadily. However, its principal function at present is as a follow-through supplement to direct mail campaigns.

Raising money through personal-acquaintance networks

Personal network solicitation is a very different form of fundraising and involves very different kinds of professional and volunteer operatives. Given the mathematical constraints imposed by the $1,000 ceiling, successful personal-acquaintance solicitation campaigns must rely on a very large number of people making the initial contacts with the potential contributors. It is therefore necessary to create an organized hierarchical structure, with central fundraisers identifying a large body of solicitors who recruit other solicitors as well as contributors. This pyramid can go down through several levels, although in most campaigns it is not more than three or four layers deep.

Campaign fundraisers whom we interviewed agree that the key to a successful personal-acquaintance pyramid operation is the small cadre of professional solicitors at the top. The first step, therefore, is to recruit top fundraisers from an existing pool of experienced solicitors in each party, although most campaigns succeed in developing the talents of novices as well.

Several professionals told us that there are approximately two dozen really experienced top fundraisers in each party who can network to raise a minimum of $100,000, and perhaps 200 to 400 others who can raise between $10,000 and $100,000.[6] Thus within the pool of contributors to each party there is a small core of very well-connected solicitors who are capable of mobilizing several hundred other solicitors.[7]

One of the earliest tasks of a successful personal-acquaintance solicitation campaign, then, is to mobilize key solicitors who will take a leave from their regular jobs (often in law firms) and spend a year making 100 to 200 phone calls a day. Although a campaign may hire a top professional to court the major solicitors, almost always these key figures will be personally wooed by the candidate, who must make the final pitch to close the deal. Early in the campaign, therefore, candidates vie for the support of the identifiable top fundraisers in their party. For instance, more than two years before the 1988 election, Bush combed the field of Republican middle-range solicitors not only to enhance his own fundraising efforts, but also to deny Dole access to these key individuals who might have supported him instead.[8] It should also be noted that some candidates solicit for contributions as well. Babbitt spent hours on the phone before the Iowa caucuses in 1988 trying to persuade those who had given serious money to raise their gift to the maximum $1,000 (Walsh 1992).

Once recruited, top solicitors then reach out to their network of associates and recruit others to solicit, often giving them quotas. A typical initial target is $10,000, which would mean identifying ten people (usually including the solicitor and members of the solicitor's own family), each of whom will give the $1,000 limit. As Robert Farmer described it, "What I do . . . is sit down with people of status, influence, and prestige and ask them to exercise their network for Michael Dukakis."[9]

Those who succeed in raising a specified amount of money are often awarded honorary titles and given other forms of social stroking commensurate with their level of accomplishment. For example, in the Dukakis campaign of 1988, there were about 900 "National Finance Committee" members who raised $10,000, 100 or more "Directors" who raised $25,000, and more than a dozen "Co-Chairs" or "Trustees" who raised $100,000. The Dukakis campaign also used "Ambassadors" from Massachusetts who went to other states to raise money or lead fundraising efforts.[10]

Pyramids typically have a reward structure that gives higher-ups differential credit both for the money they solicited personally and for that solicited through others recruited below them on the pyramid. In the Dukakis campaign, this system of gratitude-accounting was called the "Credit Line,"[11] and it seems that contributors were aware of its existence. As one contributor put it, "If you're going to give a thousand dollars, you channel it through someone so that he can get credit for it. It doesn't mean anything to me, but it might mean something to him, if he wants something later, a job or something."[12]

One major organizational technique designed to focus and structure fundraising efforts is the fundraising event, scheduled for a specific date, at which the candidate appears. Such events serve to create financial targets and time deadlines for the solicitors. They are particularly important tools at the beginning of a campaign. Not only do they serve to focus and energize early home-state fundraising activities (as was the case with Dukakis), they also assist in raising early money out of state because they provide immediate social returns in exchange for the contribution: small elite events usually provide direct access to the candidate; larger events provide the opportunity for solicitors to network with each other.

Our interviews with campaign finance professionals suggest that solicitors have different motivations from other contributors. Moreover, the mix of motives changes as one moves down the pyramid. Participants agree that the very top two dozen or so solicitors in each party are individuals who view fundraising as a profession or an all-consuming avocation. During the campaign period, fundraisers at this level are fully involved in politics, and they either make their living through political activity or have made enough money in another career so that they can devote full time to political interests. Since solicitors at all levels are subject to burnout, and some, especially at lower levels, may exhaust their networks, many of these individuals turn to other pursuits after a few years of soliciting, and others cycle in and out of full-time fundraising. Some, of course, will remain in politics for the rest of their lives.

There are several important reasons why these top solicitors sign on to a particular campaign: being approached first, the personal chemistry between the candidate and the solicitor, and strategic objectives related to a candidate's chances of winning. For example, fundraisers for long-shot candidates, swimming in a small pond, generally have more authority, latitude, and access to a candidate during the campaign – and more appreciation afterward. Moreover, there is the sheer excitement and personal challenge of raising money for a long shot, even though that candidate has a smaller chance of winning. Fundraisers for front-runners, while swimming in a larger sea, have a greater chance of gaining some access to a sitting president. Unless the candidate is a front-runner, he or she, playing to these motives, needs to be persuasive and persistent to be successful, since backing a winner is important to almost all top solicitors.

Our interviews with campaign finance professionals suggested that the motives of the second echelon of solicitors – the few hundred who can routinely raise $10,000 and more – are similar to those at the top, although there is the added motivation of their relations with the top solicitors who recruited them. These, too want to back a winner, and they, too, will typically meet the candidate personally. Each will make a substantial commitment in terms of the amount of time she or he will devote to the cause and the length of time each will donate. Most networkers at this level are unpaid and must have significant personal resources to enable them to take such a lengthy period of time away from their careers.

The higher the level of the solicitor, the greater the expectations of personal influence within the campaign and perhaps ultimately in the resultant administration. This influence is not always directed toward material gain. Some may seek to work for good public policy for its own sake; others may do so not because of their interest in policy per se, but because they wish to be known for such an accomplishment. Yet others may place great value on the perquisites of power that accompany influence on the policy agenda.

As the pyramid broadens, the expectations of personal influence diminish and the nature of the reward structure changes as well. Solicitors near the top want to back a winner in order to be a part of the group running the government; solicitors beneath them may participate to earn access to top officials for business or professional reasons, to affirm their friendship with a higher-level solicitor, to earn social recognition and develop social contacts, or for the sheer novelty of the game.

In addition, networking is based primarily on business and professional contacts.[13] This activity involves "'access' (that demure cousin of influence) to people in power, both commercial and political."[14] For example, large amounts of money in the 1970s were networked throughout the oil and gas industry; in the 1980s this occurred among property developers. As the focus of government regulatory activity shifts and economic opportunities offered by different types of business interests fluctuate, economic-interest networking changes over time.

Middle-level solicitors often seek both material and social rewards not directly associated with governmental or political matters. Not only do successful solicitors want to be invited to White House or Kennedy Center galas, but "there is a certain cachet to hosting a prospective president in one's home – and in the barely concealed knowledge that one has raised an impressive sum of money in doing so."[15] As Nadine Hack, a Dukakis fundraiser, described some solicitors, "These people: first they've conquered Wall Street, Park Avenue, and East Hampton, and now their sights are set on Washington. . . . If not for politics, . . . they would concentrate on raising money for the ballet, for their favorite hospital."[16]

The lowest levels of soliciting in the pyramid involve one individual asking his or her friends or business associates to contribute. For instance, according to several fundraising professionals interviewed for this study, this level of solicitors includes vendors and others who "can't say no" to business contacts who ask them to solicit. As Joel McCleary, Treasurer of the Democratic party under Carter, observed about Dukakis's success, "Someone who owns a Greek restaurant probably knows more people to call for $1,000 than the CEO of Texas Instruments."[17] A solicitor at this level might be asked to fill a table or a few tables at an event. A CEO might also turn to the officers in his or her corporation and ask them to contribute. Alternatively, an individual might solicit close friends in the same social network. Of course, given the nature of the pyramid, most soliciting is done at this level. In order to raise the large amounts of money necessary to fund a successful presidential campaign, the pyramid must be extremely broad at the base. Thus, most of the respondents in our survey were solicited in this fashion.

At the very bottom of the pyramid are the contributors who do not solicit. Anecdotal accounts of why they respond to personal solicitations emphasize solidary and material motives. The fundraisers we interviewed seemed in general agreement about this. Conventional wisdom holds that in personal-acquaintance networking the emphasis is truly on the personal.[18] As Ronald Brownstein explains, "For the most part . . . the forces involved are local, personal; for many . . . the decision is not whether to support Bush over Kemp or Dole . . . , but whether to reject a direct request from their friend." One wealthy individual who hosted a debt retirement fundraiser for a presidential candidate was even more explicit. He pulled the candidate aside, asked him not to make a long political speech, and added, somewhat ungraciously, "Be brief. These people aren't here for you; they are here for me. Most of them didn't even support you."

Such personal connections can arise from the same rich variety of sources that motivate people to solicit, as discussed above. In addition, there is a practice of reciprocal giving among those who give frequently to social, political, and philanthropic causes. Many people respond favorably to the approaches of solicitors because they expect those solicitors, in turn, to respond favorably in the future to their own fundraising appeals for charity or civic causes. As Nadine Hack explained after a fundraiser she hosted, "A lot of people who were there will now approach me for their various charities. Someone will send me an invitation for the cancer this, and someone else will send me an invitation for the ballet. For me to be in a position where I can write checks at their fundraisers certainly does help."[19]

In sum, participants all tend to emphasize the personal nature of networks and downplay such factors as attitudes toward the candidate, including the perceived ideological proximity of the candidate to the contributor. We should be cautious, however, in embracing this description of how the process works because it may be self-serving: key solicitors might be expected to argue that it is their own efforts and their own networking ability, not the attractiveness of the candidate, that are the key variables in raising money.

This is an important issue. Is it true, as some solicitors imply, that the internal dynamics of the solicitation process can take on a life of its own, so that serious money can be raised from large numbers of contributors on the basis of who is friendly with whom, irrespective of the attractiveness of the candidate or the positions that the candidate takes? Is the only requirement for raising serious money through a personal-acquaintance network simply to be successful in hiring those key people at the start who can activate their networks within the pool of contributors on behalf of almost anyone? If so, there are serious implications for democratic theory.

Measuring methods of solicitation

Our survey data allow us to examine the validity of these descriptive accounts of the differences in motivations that underlie the two basic fundraising techniques. We classified the contributors in our study according to how their contribution was solicited. We asked the respondents how they were *first* solicited to contribute in 1988, and our analysis throughout is based on this first solicitation – the successful "recruitment" solicitation – because that is the crucial contact for fundraisers. Many contributors who do not initially give the maximum allowable by law are later resolicited by other means, including follow-up mail, telephone, or personal contact. Respondents to our survey could indicate that they were contacted personally by someone they knew, contacted personally by someone they didn't know, contacted by mail by someone they knew, or contacted by mail by someone they didn't know.

Approximately one in four contributors of serious money in 1988 were first contacted through the mail by someone they did not know. An additional 3% were contacted personally by someone they did not know, which is principally telemarketing. Nearly three-fifths gave as a result of an initial personal solicitation by someone they knew. An additional 14% were solicited through the mail by someone they knew. This means that 72% were contacted by someone they knew personally and 28% were contacted by someone they did not know.

Three of these four types of solicitation (direct mail, telemarketing, and personal-contact networking) represent well-known methods of fundraising. The fourth category (solicitation through mail by someone the contributor knows personally) needs elaboration. Campaign finance professionals we interviewed described several types of solicitation that come under this rubric. First, there are letters from leading party figures to minor party figures on behalf of candidates. There are also letters from businesspeople to employees or others with whom they do business. In some special networks, fundraisers have developed long-term relationships with their contacts that can be activated by a simple letter. Finally, some contributors receive letters from a candidate whom they know or whom they feel they know.[20]

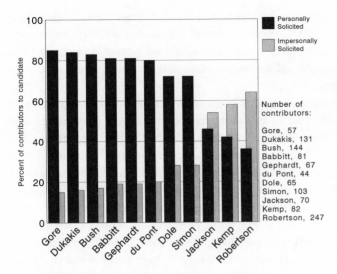

Figure 4.1. Method of solicitation by candidate.

Our analysis suggests there is a fundamental distinction between those who were first contacted by a stranger and those who were contacted by someone they knew. For these reasons we have combined those who were contacted *in person* by someone they knew and those who were contacted *through the mail* by someone they knew into a single category of personal-network solicitation. We also combined those who were contacted by a stranger through the mail or by telemarketing into a single category of impersonal solicitation.[21] The distinction between these two basic methods of solicitation is used throughout the book.

Figure 4.1 shows the percent of respondents in the two categories for each candidate's contributors. We present the data separately by candidate, though we should note that the number of respondents is large only for Bush, Dukakis, and Robertson. Between 80% and 85% of contributors to Gore, Dukakis, Bush, Babbitt, Gephardt, and du Pont were solicited by someone they knew personally, as were 72% of contributors to Dole and Simon. Only in the case of the three most ideologically extreme candidates, Jackson, Kemp, and Robertson, were less than half the contributors of serious money initially approached this way. For these three candidates, more than half were initially contacted impersonally.

These results confirm the widespread belief among campaign finance specialists that successful impersonal solicitations are likely to be made by candidates who represent the ideological wings of their party, while centrist candidates, often holding powerful public offices that facilitate networking, are more likely to mobilize solicitors who have personal contacts.These results show that personal networking dominates serious money solicitation in most campaigns.

Our data also confirm the insider status of personal-acquaintance network contributors. Compared to those impersonally solicited, personal network givers are more likely to have held party office and public appointive office. They are also more likely to have been asked by others for political advice, to have been asked by others for help with the national government, and to have helped form a new group or organization to try to solve some community problem.[22] Those solicited by mail or telemarketing are especially likely to have *written* to a policy maker, while personal-acquaintance network contributors are especially likely to have *spoken* with a policy maker. Those solicited impersonally are also more likely to have participated in demonstrations. The demographic differences fit this insider–outsider distinction: in 1988 those contributors solicited through a personal network were more likely to be better-educated, affluent, middle-aged, and male than those successfully contacted through impersonal networks.

The crucial ingredient in personal networking is the solicitors, and solicitors have an even higher insider status than personal-network contributors generally. These individuals are much more involved in virtually all types of political activity than are those who do not solicit. They are more likely to contact policy makers directly, write to policy makers, engage in group-based political activity, and take part in demonstrations. Our Index of Campaign Work shows that they are more active in campaigns as well: only 14% of those in the lowest category on this index solicit contributions from others, compared with 76% of those in the highest category.

The methods and motives

The two fundraising methods described above are not simply grounded in the FECA rules or in recent technical developments in fundraising. They also arise from the different underlying motives that contributors give for participating in politics. There is a clear relationship between motives for participation and the methods of successful solicitation. Figure 4.2 presents the importance of the different motives in 1988 for contributors initially contacted by each method. The data shown in Figure 4.2 are consistent with the descriptions provided by the campaign professionals we interviewed, which

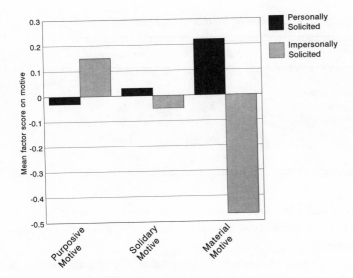

Figure 4.2. Motives by methods of solicitation.

emphasize the importance of material and solidary motives for contributors in personal networks and of purposive motives for contributors solicited by direct mail and telemarketing.

It should be noted that these relationships are due in part to the types of candidates who use each method of solicitation, but the relationships still exist among both ideological candidates and moderate candidates. We isolated those who gave to Bush, Dole, and Dukakis on the one hand (representing moderate candidates), and to Jackson, Kemp, and Robertson on the other (representing ideological candidates). The relationships shown above hold for both sets of candidates, although controlling for candidate type does reduce the magnitude of the differences somewhat. This shows that different methods of solicitation attract contributors with different political motives, regardless of the nature of a candidate's appeal. Although Figure 4.2 shows the strongest relationship between method of solicitation and material motives, it must be remembered that purposive reasons are the most important for respondents regardless of how they were solicited.

Contributors with purposive motives disproportionately hold extreme ideological views. Therefore, not surprisingly, there is a positive correlation between this motive and ideological extremism. There is also a strong relationship between methods of solicitation and extremism on a liberal–conservative scale. The data in Table 4.1 show that those contributors initially

Table 4.1. *Ideological extremism by method of solicitation*

	Personal, %	Impersonal, %
Moderate	13	4
Slightly conservative or liberal	38	20
Conservative or liberal	45	60
Extremely conservative or liberal	5	17
	100	100
	$n = 754$	$n = 302$

contacted successfully by direct mail or telemarketing are more likely to exhibit extreme ideological views than those successfully solicited through personal networks.

One way in which we can illustrate the importance of purposive motives is to determine what percent of contributors gave to the candidate the contributor perceived to be most ideologically proximate. This ideological proximity is also related to the method of initial solicitation, as shown in Table 4.2. In examining this relationship, it is fruitful to distinguish between those who are in the home state of the candidate and those who are not, for we find interesting differences between these two groups. In Table 4.2, a contributor is counted as giving to the most ideologically proximate candidate (on a seven-point liberalism–conservatism scale) if no other candidate *in the race at the time of the contribution* was perceived by the contributor to be closer to his or her own position.

Those solicited through direct mail or telemarketing were indeed more likely to give to the candidate perceived to be closest to the contributor's own position on the liberal–conservative scale than those solicited through personal networks. In addition, contributors from the home state of the candidate are consistently less likely to have given to the candidate closest to their own ideology. The difference is especially pronounced for those initially solicited through personal networks, for business and solidary benefits are more readily available in home-state personal networks as incentives to encourage contributions.

It might at first appear unusual that only 70% of contributors initially solicited by direct mail by an out-of-state candidate gave to the candidate most proximate to them. These numbers may understate the importance of purposive motivations, however. There are several possible reasons why a person may have not contributed to the ideologically most proximate candi-

Table 4.2. *Percentage of contributors giving to ideologically closest candidate, by method of solicitation*

	In-state	Out-of-state
Solicited personally	41	60
	$n = 191$	$n = 555$
Solicited impersonally	64	70
	$n = 71$	$n = 226$

date but still employed a purposive strategy in making the contribution. First, some may have given strategically, contributing to a candidate who was slightly less close to them ideologically than another but who might have had a better chance of winning either the nomination or the general election. Second, some contributors may have given to both their most proximate candidate and to another candidate, and we sampled the contribution to that latter candidate. Third, the contributor may never have been solicited by his or her most proximate candidate. Finally, differences on ideology may in a few cases be less important than proximity on a specific issue that is salient to a contributor.

Our interviews with campaign professionals, who emphasized the importance of personal relationships between the solicitor and contributor, suggest that such relationships are often far more important in successful solicitations than is the ideological proximity of the candidate. Indeed, as shown in Table 4.2, only 41% of contributors solicited by an in-state candidate through a personal network gave to the most proximate candidate. It is, however, one thing to ask whether or not the contributor is giving to the most ideologically proximate candidate; it is another thing to ask whether or not the contributor is giving to a candidate with whom he or she is in some fundamental disagreement. Although it is true that personal-network solicitation does successfully reach individuals who are not ideologically as close to a candidate as is the norm for direct mail/telemarketing solicitation, our data do not support a sweeping conclusion that the personal relationship is all-important. In fact, they suggest that contributors of serious money do not often give to candidates with whom there is a fundamental disagreement of either ideology or partisanship.

There is, in fact, only a small percentage of contributors who give across both partisan and ideological lines in our survey. In the survey as a whole,

62% gave in agreement with their partisanship and ideology, and only 7% conflicted on both.[23] However, among contributors to Democratic candidates, fully 20% identified as Republicans, and 12% gave across both party and ideological lines. As we might expect, mismatches on both partisanship and ideology are most likely to occur when the contributor was solicited in person by someone they knew personally. This is especially true when the contributor was solicited on behalf of an in-state candidate. In fact, among Republican contributors personally solicited on behalf of a home-state candidate, an astonishing 42% gave to a Democrat. These primarily Republican cross-party, cross-ideology contributors scored disproportionately high on material motives and low on solidary and purposive motives. This result provides confirmation of the observations of fundraising professionals that material motives can override partisan and policy preferences.

Conclusions

We find that presidential fundraising is conducted primarily through two methods: impersonal contact through direct mail or telemarketing, and personal contact by someone the contributor knows in a fundraising network. Contributors who respond to these methods differ in their demographic characteristics and their political activities. These techniques resonate with contributors having different mixes of motives, and vary in their value to candidates with different sets of resources.

These results, taken together, strongly suggest that there are real political constraints on the fundraising strategies each campaign can employ. This is not a case of simply hiring the right professionals and sitting back while they do their job. Nor is this simply a mechanical exercise of statistical projection. Fundraising strategies depend on a complex set of factors, including the political makeup of the contributing pool, the receptivity of its components to different types of solicitation, and the positions of candidates with respect to each other in terms of both the political landscape and the candidates' resources, broadly defined. We therefore turn to the questions of exactly what resources enable a candidate to build a financial constituency, and how that constituency is constructed.

5. Candidate resources

All serious presidential nomination campaigns must carefully assess the resources available to them that can be used to build a financial base. Although each candidate has a unique set of resources, there are five major types that were important in both 1988 and 1992, and will probably remain so in the future. These consist of having a strong home-state constituency; possessing strong ties to national party activists; exercising positions of congressional leadership or having access to the national legislative agenda; sharing ethnic, religious, or other types of social identities with major groups of potential donors; and being well-placed on the ideological spectrum. Each of these resources enables a candidate to tap into the pool of contributors and mobilize an important segment of it. Thus some candidates can take advantage of the opportunities provided by current or former political office, others build on organizational and individual relationships they have developed over the years, and still others exploit common ties of ideology and social identity with their contributors.

The presidential candidate resembles the interest-group entrepreneur of Robert Salisbury's (1969) formulation: he or she must assemble a set of "benefits" that will attract enough contributors to fund the campaign. These solidary, purposive, and material motives activate different sets of contributors and are more or less useful to different types of candidates. Like an interest-group entrepreneur, the candidate must build an organization to distribute these benefits and to attract members (contributors).

In the previous chapter, we demonstrated that there is a connection between the benefits that contributors seek and the methods that candidates use to solicit them. Potential candidates and their campaign staff must choose the financial constituency they will target, and then choose the method for soliciting its members. The intersection of these decisions by the campaign and those by the contributors creates financial constituencies.

As we showed in Chapter 3, presidential candidates generally seek to attract contributions from a relatively constant pool of presidential contributors. Some candidates can expand the pool by attracting donations from individuals who have never before given to a presidential candidate, but as we have shown, even outsider candidates such as Robertson and Jackson attracted a majority of their serious money from the pool of previous donors. Thus candidates use their resources primarily to mobilize the pool of regular contributors, and to a lesser extent to attract new contributors to their campaigns.

In this chapter we focus primarily on the five resource bases that campaigns may tap. Candidates generally hope to mobilize contributors by using one or more of these resource bases, and they do so by using the methods described in Chapter 4. The choice of method is generally related to the nature of the resource base. Both personal and impersonal solicitations can be used to mobilize in-state funds, although the largest early in-state contributions are generally raised through personal contact. Personal networks are also the major method for exploiting the resources of party, congressional office, and in many cases religious or ethnic identity. Direct mail and telemarketing are the main mechanisms that ideologically extreme candidates use to raise money from those who share their beliefs, but moderate candidates receive at least some money through personal networks because of their ideological and policy positions.

In this chapter, we examine more closely the different financial constituencies of each candidate. We confine our analysis to candidate strategies and constituencies in 1988. The 1992 survey was mailed only to those who gave in 1988, and therefore those data do not represent a random sample of contributors to the 1992 candidates. We did not survey new Arkansas contributors to Clinton, for example, or the Catholic conservatives who gave to Buchanan but did not give to Robertson or Kemp in 1988. In Chapter 6, we more closely examine contribution decisions by individuals in 1992.

Home-state contributions

The first resource that most presidential candidates mobilize is their home-state base, which forms the nucleus of their early fundraising efforts. This is especially true for candidates who are sitting or former governors, but it is true for Senators and members of Congress as well. These officeholders have lengthy lists of financial supporters from earlier campaigns. Contributors on these lists are generally concentrated in the constituency – that is, the state – of the candidate.

It might seem initially that home-state candidates could mobilize large numbers of in-state supporters new to presidential contributing. The vast majority of in-state contributors, however, are part of the contributor pool described in Chapter 3. Our analysis of in-state contributors suggests that the vast majority have given in at least some previous presidential elections, and that they are only slightly less likely than out-of-state contributors to have given at least occasionally in the past.

This in-state financial base provides seed money that helps candidates make early campaign appearances and hire the media consultants, pollsters, fundraisers, and other personnel necessary to conduct a modern campaign. As the term "seed money" suggests, early money frequently grows into more substantial sums, for the candidates spend this money to gain name recognition and to build a favorable image (Biersack, Herrnson, and Wilcox 1993). If they are successful, they then will be able to attract additional donors from outside their own state or district.

Most of the candidates in 1988 relied on home-state contributors for a substantial portion of their early receipts. This is especially true for all the former and sitting governors, but it is also true for the senators as well. This was even true for George Bush, who raised substantial sums through national networks, and for Jack Kemp, who relied primarily on direct mail to fund his campaign. Both candidates raised large amounts in their home states of Texas and New York, although these states provided early money to other candidates as well.

In-state seed money is less important for candidates with national reputations and/or large direct mail lists. In 1988, Robertson and Jackson raised most of their earliest funds outside of their home states. That these two candidates went out of state for their early monies is not surprising: both Robertson and Jackson had name recognition through national religious and civil rights organizations. Robertson and Jackson were also the only two candidates never to have held elected office within their home states, and therefore lacked a list of in-state political contributors and a network of in-state solicitors.

Candidates raise money in-state using the same methods of solicitation described in Chapter 4. They use mail and personal solicitations to reach their previous contributors. These contacts generally create immediate high returns on the resources used to make them because individuals who have supported a candidate for one office are likely to support him or her for a higher office.

As candidates move beyond their own lists, they target state party donors and activists and capitalize especially on business-related networks. Terry McAuliffe, fundraiser for the Gephardt campaign, notes that sitting governors are best positioned to raise in-state funds because they can tap firms that do business with the state and build networks among the vendors who supply those firms. Since most candidates ultimately lose their presidential bid, sitting governors may receive as much in-state money from donors who anticipate that they will lose (and will therefore remain important sources of business) than from donors who believe that the candidate will win.

Senators also have many fundraising connections from their Senate campaigns, but they are generally less able than governors to mobilize in-state money because they lack the patronage of state government. Yet their Washington offices are important resources because they have access to the national policy agenda and to the local distribution of political largesse from Washington. Thus all Senators have extensive home-state networks and lists.

Since House members almost always have smaller constituencies than Senators, they have correspondingly less leverage in raising home-state funds. In some large states they may lack name recognition beyond the reach of the major media of their district. Yet even House members rely on in-state money as seed money. McAuliffe reported that Gephardt raised approximately $1 million in Missouri, and most of this money was from his district. The campaign held many small events in the district, and it remained a steady source of funds. During the first televised primary debate, Gephardt held "house parties" in his district where contributors watched the debate, then listened to a video from the candidate. Scott MacKenzie told us that Jack Kemp also launched his campaign with a large fundraising dinner in his district in April 1987.

In general a candidate who is a statewide officeholder from a large state has a tremendous advantage in fundraising over a candidate from a small state holding the same office. For example, Pete Wilson raised $4.4 million in large donations from individual contributors in California for his 1988 Senate race. In contrast, Malcolm Wallop raised just $84,000 in large donations from his home state while winning the Senate race in Wyoming. Pete Wilson's list of contributors is clearly a much more valuable resource should he choose to run for the presidency than is Malcolm Wallop's.

The timing of in-state funds

To examine the importance of home-state contributors as a source of seed money, we use data from the Federal Election Commission (FEC), which includes the date of the contribution and address of the contributor for all gifts of $500 or more.[1] Although these data are based on a larger contribution size than those in our study, our estimates of the percentage of in-state funds raised from contributors who gave $200 or more are similar to the results obtained from these FEC data.[2]

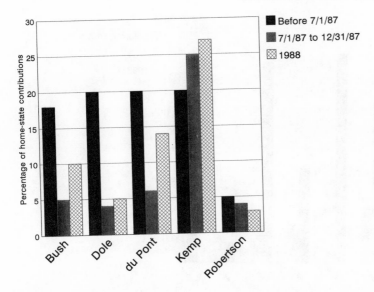

Figure 5.1. Republican home-state funds by period.

We have divided the 1988 election cycle into three periods: the period before July 1, 1987; the second half of 1987; and the 1988 campaign. During the first period, candidates raised seed money and built their campaign organizations. During the latter half of 1987, the campaigns began to broaden their fundraising efforts to qualify for matching funds. During 1988, the primary elections and caucuses brought media attention to the candidates and enabled them to raise additional monies from many different geographic areas.

Figure 5.1 shows the percentage of contributors of $500 or more who lived in the candidate's home state for Republican candidates, and Figure 5.2 shows the same information for Democratic candidates. All candidates except Jackson and Robertson raised substantial amounts of monies from within their home states during the earliest period. Bush, Dole, du Pont, and Kemp all raised approximately 20% of their earliest monies from their home states. Democratic candidates relied even more heavily on home-state funds: Gephardt raised a third of his early money from Missouri, Babbitt received more than half from Arizona, and Simon, Gore, and Dukakis each raised more than two-thirds of their large-gift seed money from their home states.[3] During the earliest months of the campaign, all candidates except Jackson and Robertson raised more money in their home states than in any other single state. This was true even for the well-funded Bush campaign, which received more than $600,000 in large gifts from early events in Houston.

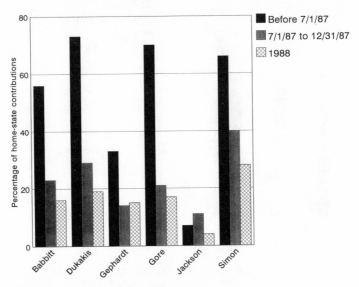

Figure 5.2. Democratic home-state funds by period.

After that initial period, the percentage of funds   m outside the candidates' home states increased sharply as they sought to qualify for matching
funds and to build a truly national campaign. Of those candidates who
raised substantial amounts of in-state monies, only Kemp increased the
proportion of his funds coming from his home state after the initial
period.[4] Other candidates relied increasingly on "money centers" such as
New York, Los Angeles, Houston, Chicago, and Miami. Ultimately both
Dole and du Pont raised more money in at least one state other than their
small home states.

Although candidates relied primarily on out-of-state money later in their
campaigns, the overall percentage of funds ultimately çoming from the candidate's home states is nonetheless impressive. Figure 5.3 summarizes the
results from the first two figures. It shows the percentage of money raised in
individual contributions of $500 or more from contributors in each candi-
date's home state throughout the campaign. The data suggest that for all
Democratic candidates except Jesse Jackson, more than one in five dollars of
these large contributions came from the home state. Dukakis raised more than
a third of his largest contributions from Massachusetts.

There are two factors that influence the amount of in-state money a candidate can raise – the size of the base and the yield. The base is the number
of affluent people willing to make contributions, if asked by the right candi-

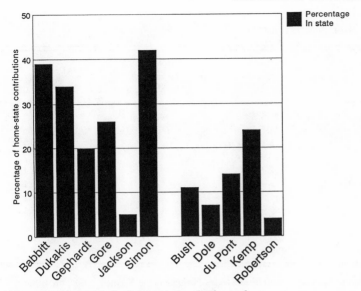

Figure 5.3. Home-state fundraising during election cycle.

date – primarily the pool of contributors who live in the state. The yield is the amount of money raised for each possible dollar that can be tapped.

One crude measure of yield is to compare the aggregate state wealth with the amount of money raised by the candidate in his home state. In Table 5.1, we provide these data. In the first columns, we provide a measure of the base – state personal income. The second column provides a measure of the amount of money raised by the home-state candidate. In the final column, we provide a measure of the yield of each candidate, or his effectiveness in mobilizing the available political money in his state. This is the total dollar value of these large contributions divided by the net income of the state.[5]

Dukakis and du Pont have the same high yield, but they differ greatly in the total amount of in-state money raised because of the different size of their state base. With identical yields Dukakis raised ten times the amount of money in-state that du Pont raised. With a far lower yield Bush raised five times the amount of in-state money as du Pont raised, because Texas is a far larger financial base than Delaware.

There are two regularities evident in Table 5.1. First, there is a correlation between types of candidates and their ability to mobilize the wealth of their state. Governors and well-established members of Congress tend to be more successful in tapping in-state wealth, and those candidates who have not held elective office are the least able to mobilize in-state funds. The low

Table 5.1. *Home-state effort*

	State personal income[a]	Money raised in $500 contributions	Yield
Dukakis (MA)	122.6	4,376	35.7
du Pont (DE)	11.7	417	35.6
Dole (KS)	39.3	757	19.3
Gore (TN)	67.9	1,170	17.2
Babbitt (AZ)	52.2	575	11.1
Gephardt (MO)	79.4	723	9.1
Bush (TX)	245.6	2,006	8.2
Simon (IL)	189.9	1,000	5.3
Kemp (NY)	345.7	771	2.2
Robertson (VA)	106.3	94	0.9
Jackson (IL)	189.9	80	0.4

[a]Income received from all sources by residents of candidate home state for 1988 (in billions).
Source: 1990 Statistical Abstract of U.S., p. 436.

yields for Kemp and Simon also suggest that it is not simply the lack of elective office but also ideological extremism that either hampers home-state fundraising or diverts efforts from it because national direct mail fundraising is more attractive.

In addition, there is a negative correlation between the net wealth of a state and the ability of a candidate to mobilize that wealth. Although in absolute dollars, coming from a large, wealthy state is obviously an advantage, candidates from such states typically raise a smaller portion of that wealth in contributions than those from less affluent states. The single, but very important, exception to this rule was Dukakis, who was the most successful candidate in raising in-state funds by this measure.

Another measure of in-state fundraising success is the percentage of contributions the home-state candidate receives out of all contributions from that state made to candidates of his party. Most candidates succeeded in mobilizing most of the available early political money in their home states. The ability to shut out other candidates, however, does not necessarily translate into raising large sums in-state. Dole was the recipient of 85% of Republican contributions from Kansas during the seed money period, but this provided his campaign with only slightly more than $400,000. In contrast Bush got 74% of the earliest Republican contributions from Texas, but this amounted to nearly $1.4 million because of the large base.

For the Democrats, a similar pattern is evident in the data. Dukakis, Gephardt, and Gore each received more than 98% of the earliest contributions from their home states going to Democratic candidates. These percentages are quite impressive, suggesting a very successful effort to corral in-state political funds. Yet this similar success had very different payouts – less than $350,000 for Gephardt, less than $725,000 for Gore, and more than $2.2 million for Dukakis. Paul Simon was somewhat less successful in cornering the early Democratic money from Illinois, receiving only 75% of these funds. Yet this amounted to more money than Gephardt raised in Missouri.

It should be remembered that Gephardt and also Kemp were members of the House and their elective constituency constituted only a portion of their states. They both raised substantial portions of their in-state money from within their congressional district, with presumably high yields. Approximately 70% of Gephardt's in-state large donations came from St. Louis alone, not including the suburbs and the rural areas of his district. Gephardt's difficulties stemming from the size of his in-state base can be seen in comparing his earliest receipts to those of Dukakis. Outside of their home states, Gephardt and Dukakis raised similar amounts of money ($700,000 for Gephardt, $800,000 for Dukakis) in the first period. Yet Dukakis had a $1.9 million advantage in home-state funds, and this advantage was nearly twice the total receipts of Gephardt during that period.[6]

The Dukakis home-state effort

The most impressive home-state effort in either party was that of the Dukakis campaign. He had the highest yield, and building upon a moderately large base, his campaign raised more than twice the dollar totals in-state of any other candidate. The campaign created a "house file" for direct mail from those who had contributed to Dukakis's gubernatorial campaigns, and it mailed to that list every twenty-two days. More important, the campaign built networks of in-state solicitors who asked friends, colleagues, and business associates to contribute to the Dukakis campaign. As was typical of the 1988 home-state campaigns, most of Dukakis's fundraising was based on personal networks. Indeed, 81% of the home-state Dukakis contributors in our sample were initially solicited by someone they knew personally.

Dukakis's in-state network included many enthusiastic supporters. He built on the party network in Massachusetts and attracted contributions from Greek Americans through his shared ethnicity. He networked successfully among a large number of in-state Jewish contributors as well. Some of these individuals were motivated by solidary benefits, and many, especially those solicited impersonally, were motivated by purposive goals as well.

As we discussed in Chapter 4, the material motive is also an important part of personal networking, and our data show this was important in the Dukakis home-state campaign. Although at least one of Dukakis's top fundraisers stated that solicitors were told not to approach individuals who did business with the state for contributions, several newspaper and other articles attested to the extensive solicitation of executives of firms who did business with the state of Massachusetts, or of members of law firms who represented these clients. Many of these businesspersons in turn solicited their vendors and other associates. If instructions were given to avoid such people, it is clear that they were not successfully implemented; it may be quite difficult for top solicitors to control the behavior of lower solicitors in a large network with many levels of participants.

Barry Werth (1988) described the Dukakis in-state networks in some detail. The campaign was very successful in constructing corporate networks, including one at Fidelity Investments of Boston, where the chair and principal owner contributed along with more than fifty other executives and spouses. The contributors described by Werth were not necessarily enthusiastic backers of Dukakis for president. Charles Brennick, who owned a nursing home chain in Boston, contributed as part of a $9,000 gift (including several gifts from his children). Werth quotes Brennick as stating a strong Republican preference and as having raised money for Reagan and Bush. But Dukakis's state health care reform package affected Brennick's business, and he desperately wanted an amendment to the bill.

Overall, more than one in four of Dukakis's in-state contributors voted for Bush in 1988. This was not unusual, for other Democratic candidates also attracted a substantial number of in-state Republican contributors. In each case, these contributors generally were not strong supporters of the candidate: they rated the candidate significantly "cooler" on feeling thermometers than did Democrats who contributed to the candidate. In-state networks are successful in gaining contributions from some who do not support the candidate to whom they give. For all the candidates who had a substantial home-state effort, purposive goals were less important in the home state than in the rest of the country, and material and solidary benefits were more important.

Party differences in home-state fundraising

Democratic candidates in 1988 relied more heavily on in-state funds; Republican candidates built more national campaigns. This may be a partisan difference, but it may also be an accident of the type of candidates running in 1988. The Republican candidates generally had access to national networks or large direct mail lists. George Bush had a national network of party contributors as the sitting vice president and former party chairman, and he was able to raise substantial sums in the major money centers early in his campaign. Bush raised far more early money than Dole or Kemp in Miami, New York, and Los Angeles, presumably because of his preexisting party network.[7] Dole was able to mobilize his network of corporate lobbyists later in the campaign, and to raise money throughout the country. Although du Pont had a very high yield in Delaware, ultimately the base was too small to fund a national campaign, and he built on his business, family, and friendship ties in many northeastern states. Kemp and Robertson lacked the resources to construct an in-state campaign, so they used direct mail to tap ideological contributors.

In contrast, the Democratic candidates lacked the national reputations and resources that might enable them to put together national networks, so they were forced to rely more heavily on in-state funds. This was especially true for the losing candidates, but it was even true for Dukakis. As he gained momentum, Dukakis was increasingly able to raise funds from money centers such as Miami, Los Angeles, and Chicago, but early in the campaign he lacked the national reputation to raise substantial sums outside of Massachusetts.

To determine if the party differences in 1988 were due to the candidate mix or to the nature of the candidates, we performed an analysis on large contributions to presidential candidates in 1992. For the 1992 election cycle, the FEC entered all gifts of more than $200 into their database, and the following analysis is based on this somewhat lower threshold.[8] As noted above, the 1992 campaign was slower to materialize because of Bush's seemingly prohibitive early popularity, and only two candidates raised money in the first six months of 1991. Paul Tsongas raised approximately 61% of his $415,000 in this period from Massachusetts donors, and Douglas Wilder raised 56% of his $114,000 from Virginia contributors.

The other candidates began their fundraising efforts during the latter half of 1991, which meant that they needed to assemble a national fundraising apparatus more quickly to qualify for matching funds. Bill Clinton raised approximately one-third of his receipts from large donations during this period from Arkansas, and this provided him with nearly a million dollars. Kerrey raised approximately a quarter of his $1.3 million from Nebraska, Tsongas raised 45% of his $280,000 from Massachusetts, Wilder raised 40%

of his $314,000 from Virginia, and Bush raised 22% of his $8.1 million from Texas. Harkin's direct mail operation raised primarily out-of-state money, with only 9% coming from Iowa.

During the campaign in 1992, the percentage of in-state money dropped for all candidates as the season unfolded. We interpret these data to suggest that the pattern observed in 1988 may be generalizable – candidates rely more heavily on in-state money early in the campaign, then move to the money centers or to direct mail to provide later funds.

These 1992 candidacies reveal patterns of party differences similar to those of 1988. Most Democratic candidates raised significant sums in-state, while the two Republican candidates did not. Yet the Republican field was small and Harkin did not rely on in-state money. We believe that the candidate differences in 1988 and 1992 are not fundamentally partisan in nature. Instead, candidates from the ideological wings of their party frequently lack the resources to build large in-state networks and generally rely on their ideological identity to raise money through direct mail and telemarketing. Other candidates find more rewarding opportunities in mobilizing the national networks that they have already constructed. In 1988 and 1992 all Republican candidates fit into one of these two categories, while few Democratic candidates did so. There are Republican governors, however, who have been mentioned as presidential prospects for 1996, and they would commence their campaigns with in-state networks.

For candidates of both parties, however, the first imperative of presidential nomination finance is to raise as much money as possible from whatever source is available. Naturally most candidates will turn to their own states first in the quest for funds. With gubernatorial and senatorial contests in some large states now costing more than $10 million, clearly the financial base exists for presidential candidates from large states to raise a substantial percentage of their funds at home from their own existing networks. This creates a significant advantage for large-state officeholders over those from small states. Holding office, especially the governorship, in a large state is an important financial resource for presidential hopefuls, just as it was an important political resource in the era when party leaders effectively nominated candidates at the conventions.

Party, congressional office, and social identity

Some candidates have special ties to party loyalists, have access to special resources associated with their congressional positions, or can hope to attract

contributors based on special appeals to ethnic, religious, or other social identities. What all these resources have in common is that they are relatively
easy to exploit through national networks of personal solicitation. Of course,
some contributors in the candidate's home state are also attracted by these
resources, and some who are contacted through direct mail respond because
of them. Yet we will see below that the distinctiveness of the financial constituencies of the candidates who possess these resources is clearer among
those who gave through national networks of personal solicitation than
among the larger set of individuals who give to these candidates.

These networks are easy to build for several reasons. Party loyalists are
readily identifiable contributors, who routinely give to candidates for all levels of office and to party committees, and who may work for campaigns and
parties as well. Although a few may hold party or appointive office, national
party networks rely primarily on sets of regular party contributors who may
enjoy the solidary benefits of $1,000-a-plate dinners. Because most presiden-
tial hopefuls crisscross the country speaking at fundraisers for other political
figures well in advance of the election season, many contributors in a national
party network will have had some personal contact with a candidate in
advance of the campaign. This form of contact, however brief, still facilitates
the building of a network of supporters.

Networks based on congressional office are more easily formed by those
members with significant access to the congressional agenda. Lobbyists, PAC
donors, and others who seek benefits from Congress may give to congressional
candidates seeking the presidency not because they strongly desire the election
of these candidates, but because a contribution to a presidential campaign may
help guarantee access should the member remain in the legislature. Thus rank-
ing members of Congress can easily build national networks of contributors
among a wide range of interest groups.

Networks based on religious, ethnic, and social identities are only slightly
more difficult to build. Dukakis (and later Tsongas) asked Greek businesspeople to solicit their colleagues. Jackson had African American preachers
and other activists solicit their friends. Robertson also networked among religious activists, although mail solicitation was a far more important source of
funds for him. A large network of Jewish contributors has existed for many
years, mobilized primarily by mail solicitations by personal acquaintances
(Levick-Segnatelli, 1994).

It is important to note that party, congressional office, and social identity
are not the only bases for national networks. There are many potential routes
for such networks to develop. As solicitors enlist still other solicitors, the

potential sources of money within a network expand, and thus the networks of most 1988 candidates branched in myriad ways. However, these three resources appear to be the basis for the vast majority of national networks that have been constructed in postreform presidential elections, and they encompass the core networking activity of the 1988 candidates well.

The 1988 survey data show that national networks are more extensive among candidates who have at least one of these three resources. In Table 5.2, we show the percentage of all contributors to each candidate who were part of a national network. We define members of national networks as those who gave in response to a personal solicitation and who did not live in the home state of the candidate to which they gave. The data show that Bush and Dole solicited more than 70% of their serious money contributors through national networks, and du Pont, Dukakis, Gephardt, and Gore solicited more than 50% of theirs this way. This is not surprising, for Bush had served as party chairman, Dole, Gephardt, and Gore were all important players on Capitol Hill; and Dukakis had important ties to the Greek and Jewish communities. Candidates who represented the ideological wings of their parties and who raised substantial sums through direct mail (Kemp, Robertson, and Jackson) had fewer contributors initially solicited by personal contact.

In addition, we asked contributors if they solicited others on behalf of a candidate. These data are shown in the second column of Table 5.2. More than 40% of those who were contacted by Bush's national network asked others for money, while fewer than a third of those contacted by Dole's and Gore's networks did so. Indeed, more than half of the members of Bush's network who were contacted in person asked others to give. Although those contacted through national networks constitute a relatively small percentage of Simon's total, nearly half of these contributors in turn solicited, suggesting that Simon did build at least a rudimentary national network.

Party and congressional office as resources

Networks based on party and congressional office are constants in American electoral politics. In virtually every seriously contested presidential nomination contest, one or more candidates has built networks on these resources. In Table 5.3 we show candidate differences in the percentage of respondents who appear to have been activated by party and congressional office. We include a variety of items that measure various aspects of these resources. For each item, the first column includes all contributors to the candidate, and the second includes only those in that candidate's national network. Candidates

Table 5.2. *National networks in 1988: An overview*

	Part of Network[a], %	Solicited Others[b], %
Republicans		
Bush	71	44
Dole	70	30
du Pont	56	–
Kemp	37	–
Robertson	34	34
Democrats		
Babbitt	48	36
Dukakis	52	42
Gephardt	50	45
Gore	53	31
Jackson	43	–
Simon	47	48

"–" indicates fewer than 35 cases.
[a]Percentage of all contributors to a candidate who were solicited by someone they knew personally and who did not live in the candidate's home state.
[b]Percentage of those in the first column who solicited others.

for whom we have a very small number of national network respondents are excluded; these are typically candidates who relied on impersonal solicitations for the bulk of their fundraising. Even with this precaution, our sample sizes are relatively small for some candidates, and so our inferences must be tentative.[9] Yet our results are quite consistent with the information gathered in in-depth interviews with fundraisers for various campaigns.

The percentages based on national networks show clearer distinctions among candidates than the percentages based on all contributors, and this is especially true for the various indicators of the party resource. It appears that Bush and Simon tapped into a network of regular party contributors who give to parties in most elections. Fully 67% of Simon's national network and 63% of Bush's were regular contributors to political parties – a figure 20% higher than for any other candidate. Yet Bush's and Simon's national networks differed in that a greater number of those who gave to Simon were also party workers.

These data are consistent with descriptions of the campaigns. Phil Smith, who helped direct the Republican National Committee (RNC) fundraising efforts in 1988, told us that Bush relied heavily on regular party contributors,

Table 5.3. *The sources of national networks: Party and congressional office*

| | Partisan Measures | | | | | |
| | Give to parties in most elections | | Work for parties in most elections | | Party official | |
	All,%	NatNet,%	All,%	NatNet,%	All,%	NatNet,%
Republicans						
Bush	58	63	21	27	21	21
Dole	47	44	20	19	19	19
du Pont	34		8			
Kemp	45		11			
Robertson	26		5			
Democrats						
Babbitt	36	37	16	15	20	21
Dukakis	34	42	15	21	17	19
Gephardt	37	43	19	19	25	36
Gore	36	29	16	15	21	21
Jackson	32		16		12	
Simon	55	67	31	41	20	36

| | Congressional Measures | | | |
| | Give to PACs in most elections | | Give to exactly 1 PAC | |
	All,%	NatNet,%	All,%	NatNet,%
Republicans				
Bush	29	35	24	27
Dole	44	47	43	44
du Pont	26		22	
Kemp	30		31	
Robertson	14		23	
Democrats				
Babbitt	29	40	21	32
Dukakis	24	32	16	16
Gephardt	28	35	15	9
Gore	25	23	31	28
Jackson	11		14	
Simon	32	49	25	20

The percentages in the "All" columns are based on all contributors to each candidate. Those in the "NatNet" columns are based only on those who contributed to the candidate through national networks. Percentages are omitted for those candidates with fewer than 20 respondents.

especially on his personal list of 10,000 to 30,000 people with whom he had once made contact. Presumably Bush's longtime experience in the party, including tenure as party chair in 1973–74, helped him cement many personal friendships among party contributors.

Gephardt also built regional party networks focusing on Southern party officials. Table 5.3 shows that 36% of Gephardt's national network held party positions, a figure matched only by contributors to Simon. Terry McAuliffe, who headed Gephardt's fundraising operation, told us that Gephardt had difficulty building networks or holding events in the key money centers such as Los Angeles and New York because the odds of his winning seemed long. Instead, his campaign contacted party and elected officials in Southern states and built networks among those who regularly contributed to politics but who had not "played presidential" before. Gephardt held thirty events in Mississippi, many in towns that had never seen presidential candidates. His first contacts in these towns were the local Democratic officials.

Thus the Bush and Simon campaigns were more successful in establishing ties to national party networks than were the campaigns of any other candidates. Gephardt was successful in establishing ties to an important regional party network. In all three cases, the networks activated by these candidates contained a high proportion of contributors who were willing to solicit others to contribute. It therefore appears that party networks are especially fertile grounds for building pyramids of personal-network solicitors.

Some candidates also mobilized networks from outside of their party. Gephardt, and to a lesser extent Dukakis and Gore, mobilized networks that enabled them to receive money from Republicans.[10] Nearly one in four of those in Gephardt's network had voted Republican in the last four presidential elections, including 1988. The regular Republican voters who gave to these Democratic candidates disproportionately cited business reasons or a sense of personal obligation for participating in politics. Most also gave to Republican candidates. Thus Gephardt mobilized networks that included both a sizable number of regional Democratic party officials and a sizable number of Republicans.

Dole and to a lesser extent Gephardt built networks that were based on their positions in Congress. Dole was Senate Minority leader at the time, and it seemed clear to Washington insiders that Gephardt was destined for an important leadership position in the House. Whether or not either one became president, giving to their campaigns was likely to be an important route of access to a powerful elected official.

Yet despite their seemingly similar resource of congressional power, Dole and Gephardt attracted different types of contributors to their networks. Many of Dole's contributors gave in nearly all elections to PACs, but they are truly distinctive in giving to exactly one PAC. We think it likely that these contributors gave solely to their corporate PAC. Our interviews suggested that Dole developed a cadre of Washington-based solicitors who first approached corporate leaders.[11] These leaders in turn solicited their executives, their contractors, their suppliers, and other business contacts. Dole's contributors were largely rank-and-file PAC donors, not lobbyists. Interestingly, the percentage of Dole contributors who solicited others to give was noticeably lower than the percentage for Bush, Simon, and Gephardt. The corporate PAC givers who constituted an important part of Dole's financial constituency were willing to make a contribution to him but were much less willing to solicit others to do so. Once they wrote their check, they did not feel obliged to do anything else.

The percentage of Gephardt's national network who gave to PACs is not distinctive, primarily because of the diverse nature of a network that combined party officials and lobbyists. His network appears to have included not rank-and-file PAC contributors, but lobbyists and PAC directors. Gephardt's congressional network began with sympathetic young Democrats in the House, who contacted the lobbyist/lawyers who regularly aided their own campaigns. In the 1992 survey, we asked contributors to indicate their occupation. More than one in four of the respondents whom we had sampled as giving to Gephardt in 1988 indicated that they were lobbyists, although the number of respondents was too small for confident estimation. Thus even within party and especially congressional networks there is a high degree of heterogeneity resulting from different candidate resources and campaign decisions.

In Table 5.4 we show the differences in the motives of those who gave to various candidates, first among all contributors and then among those who gave through the candidates' national networks. The results suggest that various candidates offered different incentives for involvement in their networks, and that a different mix of motives may have been relevant for in-state contributors and those in national networks. The Dukakis national network is distinctive in the importance of solidary motives, presumably because of the use of recognition to reward solicitors. Simon's contributors are also distinctive in their solidary motivations, although this was true only for those from Illinois. Not surprisingly, those who gave to Robertson, Kemp, and Jackson were motivated by purposive concerns.

Table 5.4. *Motives for giving to national networks*

	Purposive		Solidary		Material	
	All	NatNet	All	NatNet	All	NatNet
Republicans						
Bush	-.00	.07	-.02	-.05	.18	.31
Dole	-.21	-.12	-.02	.01	.08	.46
du Pont	-.28	.04	-.24	-.31	-.10	.12
Kemp	.33	.43	-.22	-.24	-.26	.27
Robertson	.38	.32	-.20	-.07	-.50	-.46
Democrats						
Babbitt	.05	.34	.02	-.01	.10	.28
Dukakis	-.10	-.12	.18	.38	.07	.21
Gephardt	-.15	-.10	-.05	-.17	.42	.61
Gore	-.05	.09	.02	.20	.44	.36
Jackson	.38	.32	.01	.09	-.46	-.18
Simon	.10	.25	.33	.03	-.14	.10
Regularly give to:						
Parties, not PACs		.05		.23		-.14
PACs, not parties		.16		-.47		.39

Numbers shown are mean factor scores for each motive. The motives are described initially in Chapter 3. The factor scores in the "All" columns are based on all contributors to each candidate. Those in the "NatNet" columns are based only on those who contributed to the candidate through national networks.

We would expect that those contributors who are attracted to candidates because of their access to the congressional agenda would be relatively less motivated by purposive concerns and more motivated by material concerns. The data confirm this expectation. The national networks of Gephardt and Dole were distinctive in the lack of interest their contributors showed in the electoral success of the candidates. Both networks were relatively highly motivated by material concerns, but there was a subtle difference in the frequency of responses to the items that contribute to the material factor. Gephardt's lobbyists were motivated primarily by business concerns, while Dole's corporate executives were as likely to say that their political activity was expected of them as they were to say that they were motivated by business concerns.

At the bottom of Table 5.4, to highlight some of the differences between the party and congressional networks, we isolate those members of the national networks of all candidates who regularly gave to parties but not to PACs, and those who gave regularly to PACs but not to parties. Those who gave regularly to parties were more likely to be motivated by solidary benefits, while those who gave to PACs were more likely to be motivated by business concerns. Neither group was especially likely to be motivated by purposive considerations, but a closer look suggests a more subtle difference. Those who gave to parties but not PACs were more likely to be motivated by a desire to influence the outcome of an election, while those who gave to PACs but not parties were more likely to be motivated by a desire to influence public policy. This result is sensible, for parties seek to elect candidates, while PACs seek to advance the narrow economic interests or broader ideological program of their sponsoring organization. Thus it appears that party networks are more likely than those based on congressional office to involve purposive and solidary benefits, while those based on congressional office are more likely primarily to dispense material benefits.

Thus we see the resource of ties to national party activists and of congressional office being used to mobilize two very important, but quite different, networks of contributors who are first approached by someone they know personally. The resource of access to national party activists produces a network of financial supporters motivated more by solidary and purposive motives, and it is a politically more active group. The resource of congressional office, though often effective in mobilizing financial support, produces a network less politically active and more motivated by economic self-interest.

Social identity as a resource

Although party ties and congressional offices are resources that are evident in most presidential elections, other resources are also easily exploited by national networks. Racial, ethnic, and religious identities are important sources of political money, and lend themselves to the construction of national networks. Since these networks depend upon the ability of a candidate or solicitor to appeal to the issues and social identities that motivate these individuals, the importance of specific networks varies over time. In 1988 and again in 1992, candidates used racial and ethnic ties and religious affiliations to build or tap into national networks.

Although we included no direct measure of ethnicity in our survey, we did ask one open-ended question on religious affiliation. Nearly one in eight of Dukakis's national network contributors identified as Greek Orthodox; this figure doubtlessly underestimates the role of Greeks in his national networks, since some contributors of Greek ancestry would claim other religious affiliation. Dukakis was equally successful in attracting money from Greeks within Massachusetts. Our 1992 data include only fifteen Greek Orthodox respondents who had earlier given to Dukakis, but nearly all of them gave to Paul Tsongas, another candidate of Greek ancestry, confirming the anecdotal evidence that Tsongas solicited the same Greek networks as Dukakis.

An even higher proportion of the contributors to Dukakis's national networks were Jewish. Nearly one in three of those who gave to Dukakis's national networks listed their religious affiliation as Jewish, and Jews constituted a sizable percentage of the national networks of Babbitt and Gore as well. Among Dukakis givers, these two ethnic channels were mobilized at different points in the campaign. Greek givers were a major source of early Dukakis money, while Jewish contributors were relatively more important later in the campaign, especially after the race narrowed to one between Dukakis and Jackson.

Approximately one third of Jackson's contributors contacted through national networks were black. Many were probably first solicited in church, for many black churches and pastors were active parts of the Jackson fundraising efforts (Wilcox 1990). In 1991, Virginia's Governor Wilder launched a short-lived presidential bid and solicited a national network of members of his African American college fraternity.

Although large networks based on ethnic, racial, or religious characteristics often are a consequence of shared identity between the candidate and the contributor, this need not be the case for small networks. A candidate may recruit a fundraiser using purposive or material benefits, for example, and this individual may build a small network among those who share his or her own ethnic, racial, or religious identity. The individuals who contribute to such a network may have mixed motives, but many do contribute because of a sense of group identification and group goals. The fundraisers we interviewed reported that a variety of ethnic networks existed in both parties, in which the social identity of the solicitor helped cement the contribution. Phil Smith reported, for example, that Bush raised $1 million from a network of Korean Americans in 1988, and that he raised a similar amount in 1992 from another group of Asian Americans, those whose origins were in India. Terry McAuliffe showed us a *Time Magazine* cover that pictured him wrestling an alligator in an effort to win more money for Jimmy Carter from a network of Seminole Native Americans in Florida. Clinton's inroads into the Cuban financial network were widely reported in the media.

Robertson raised most of his money from mail solicitations of the regular donors to his television program (Wilcox 1991), and his contributors were disproportionately members of charismatic and pentecostal churches.[12] His constituency was narrowly focused and religious doctrine was a major source of his support.[13]

Multivariate analysis of national networks

The resources we have described in this section are best mobilized through national networks of personal solicitation. The subtle differences revealed in the bivariate analysis above are very consistent with the anecdotal evidence from campaign professionals. We wish to examine whether these distinctions are valid for national networks with multivariate controls. We have limited our analysis to contributors to the national networks of Bush and Dole in the Republican party and contributors to the national networks of Babbitt, Dukakis, Gephardt, Gore, and Simon in the Democratic party, because they are the only candidates with large national networks in 1988. For those who gave to the national networks of Bush or Dole, we estimated a logistic regression equation to predict candidate choice. For those who gave to any of the five Democrats, we used discriminant analysis to predict candidate choice. We do not show the results in tabular form.

Although we estimated a number of equations, the most parsimonious one for the Republicans contained just two variables: frequency of giving to party committees and whether the respondent gave to at least one PAC in 1988 – thus confirming the bivariate analyses that pointed to the distinction between Bush's party-based network and Dole's largely business-oriented interest-group network. The model correctly predicted approximately 79% of the cases: 71% of those who gave to Dole and 82% of those who gave to Bush. It is interesting to note that none of the other models, with a variety of additional independent variables, improved much on this baseline. Indeed, of a dozen independent variables that appeared in various equations, only sex was occasionally statistically significant, with Dole's business-based networks more male than Bush's party-based pyramid.

We also estimated a series of discriminant analyses, to distinguish among those contributors who gave to national networks of different Democratic candidates. The results suggest Gore's network was younger and more liberal than Gephardt's, that Gephardt's network had more Republicans than the networks of other Democratic candidates, and that Dukakis's national network was distinctive only in that it contained far more Greeks than did the other Democratic networks. Our analysis did provide some evidence of the distinction between national networks based on party and on congressional office, although the divisions were not as clear as those between Bush and Dole. Those who gave to Simon were somewhat more active in party campaigning than those who gave to Gephardt and Gore, while those who gave to Gephardt were more motivated by material motives than those who gave to Simon. Overall, the Democratic networks were less distinctive than the Republican networks, for all five candidates involved local party officials, all five attracted some money from Republicans, all five included contributors who cared a good deal about the outcome of the election and some who did not, and all four included liberals, moderates, and conservatives.

We conclude, therefore, that national networks based on personal association branch in myriad ways depending on the resources and connections of the candidates and of their principal fundraisers. National networks are important sources of fundraising for moderate candidates, and like in-state networks, they can raise money even from those who do not support the candidate or share his or her ideological views.

Ideology

The ideological proximity of a candidate to a potential supporter is a long-recognized political resource. Indeed, the assumption that ideological proximity is a source of political support underlies whole schools of political analysis. Candidates hope to attract contributors based on their package of issue positions. Moderate and more extreme candidates alike may receive contributions because of their ideology, as contributors identify those candidates closest to their own positions. Ideologically extreme candidates mobilize support through direct mail and telemarketing, but we show in Chapter 6 that ideology plays a role in personal networks for moderate candidates as well. For this reason, we explore the role of ideology in candidate financial constituencies broadly, and do not confine our analysis to candidates from the ideological wings of their parties or to contributors solicited impersonally. Contributors who give based on ideology must assess the policy views of candidates, and we discuss those decisions more fully in Chapter 6. In this chapter, we consider the role of ideological positions as a resource in attracting campaign funds.

If ideology is an important resource, contributors must be able to identify candidates who share their policy views. For this to occur, contributors must possess a degree of ideological sophistication that is lacking in the mass electorate. In the 1984 National Election Study (NES) data, for example, fewer than 45% of respondents correctly identified Ronald Reagan as a strong con-

Table 5.5. *Contributor perceptions of candidate liberalism–conservatism and contributor self-placement on liberalism–conservatism scale*

	Mean candidate placement	Mean contributor placement
1988 Republicans		
Bush	5.34	5.36
Dole	5.20	5.10
du Pont	5.21	5.13
Kemp	5.94	5.92
Robertson	6.11	6.03
1992 Republicans		
Bush	5.29	na
Buchanan	6.57	na
1988 Democrats		
Babbitt	2.92	3.10
Dukakis	2.32	3.18
Gephardt	3.32	3.97
Gore	3.40	3.88
Jackson	1.34	2.10
Simon	2.23	2.41
1992 Democrats		
Brown	1.61	na
Clinton	3.15	na
Harkin	2.19	na
Kerrey	2.75	na
Tsongas	3.35	na

Mean placement of each candidate on the 7-point liberalism–conservatism scale is by contributors who gave to those in the same party as the candidate, but not to the candidate himself. Mean contributor liberalism–conservatism is based on the respondent's self-placement. Both placements use the 7-point liberal–conservative scale with a range of 1 to 7 and a midpoint of 4.
na = contributors for 1992 candidates not available.

servative in the November postelection survey, despite the fact that the survey was conducted at the end of a campaign in which Reagan frequently used just that label. Fully 11% were unable to use any label to classify Reagan, and another 20% labeled him as a liberal or moderate. If we assume that those who rated him as liberal were guessing, and that a similar number guessed right and guessed wrong, then only half of respondents knew that Reagan was a conservative.

Yet contributors are a select political group and are capable of making relatively sophisticated ideological judgments. For example, contributors' ratings of the candidates closely resemble the ratings provided by a panel of political scientists surveyed by John Kessel.[14] In Table 5.5, we show the mean placement of each candidate on the seven-point liberalism–conservatism scale by contributors who gave to those in the same party as the candidate, but not to the candidate himself. In this table and in the remainder of this discussion, we are interested in a simple ordering of the candidates on ideology, and thus we have not made the corrections for measurement errors that would allow us to make a more precise estimate of candidate position. The entry of 5.34 for Bush in 1988 represents the mean rating of Bush on a liberal–conservative scale by those who gave to Dole, du Pont, Kemp, and Robertson. The second column shows the average ideological self-placement of the contributors to each candidate on this same scale. These data show that the mean ideological position of Bush's contributors was 5.36, nearly identical to the mean placement of Bush on the scale. We do not include data in this column for 1992 candidates, because we do not have a full sample of 1992 contributors.

The data in the first column of Table 5.5 show that contributors perceived that the 1988 Republican nomination was a contest between three moderate candidates – Bush, Dole, and du Pont – and two conservatives – Kemp and Robertson. In 1992, contributors perceived that Buchanan was far more conservative than Bush. Among those who gave to Democrats, contributors in 1988 saw Jackson as the most liberal candidate, followed at some distance by Simon and then Dukakis. Gore and Gephardt were perceived as the most conservative among the Democrats. In 1992, Brown was seen as clearly the most liberal, followed by Harkin. Clinton and Tsongas were seen as the most conservative Democrats.

We draw two conclusions from these data. First, contributors are relatively sophisticated in their ordering of candidate ideo-logy (see Powell 1989 for an analysis of congressional contributors). Overall, contributors with Democratic partisanship placed Dukakis at a mean of 2.43 on the liberal–conservative scale, very close to the 2.40 that John Kessel reported as the placement by the group of political scientist experts. Republicans placed Bush at 5.35, slightly to the right of the 5.20 rating of the experts. Second, the mean ideology of contributors tracks quite well with the average placement of the candidate to whom they gave. This suggests that members of the contributing pool do consider candidate ideology in deciding which candidates to support. The exceptions are primarily Republican contributors who gave to Democratic candidates. These Republicans were more conservative than Democrats who gave to these candidates, and they skew the mean considerably. This results in a poorer match between contributor and candidate ideology.

Table 5.6. *Candidate extremism and ideological proximity*

	Rated as extremely liberal or conservative by contributors to:		
	Other candidates in party	Same candidate	Average distance
1988 Republicans			
Bush			0.89
Dole			0.78
du Pont	11%	7%	0.97
Kemp	30%	25%	0.63
Robertson	59%	36%	0.37
1988 Democrats			
Babbitt			0.85
Dukakis	15%	14%	1.44
Gephardt			1.27
Gore			1.36
Jackson	73%	44%	0.62
Simon	27%	17%	1.04

Average distance is the difference between where the contributors to the candidate placed themselves and where they placed the candidate.
For purposes of presentation, only cells with at least 5% are shown.

The data in Table 5.5 show that contributors perceived that Robertson, Jackson, Kemp, and to a lesser extent Simon were the most ideologically extreme of the candidates in 1988. In Table 5.6, we show additional evidence that these four candidates were judged by the contributor pool to be the most extreme. The first column shows the percentage of contributors to other candidates of the same party who rated the candidate as extremely liberal (for Democrats) or extremely conservative (for Republicans). For the purpose of presentation, we show data only for the candidates rated as extreme by at least 5% of these respondents. A majority of other party contributors rated Robertson and Jackson as extreme, as did a substantial minority for Kemp and Simon. In our analysis below we consider these to be the candidates from the ideological wings of their parties.[15]

The second column in Table 5.6 shows the percentage of contributors to each candidate who rated that candidate as extremely conservative or extremely liberal. Substantial percentages of those who gave to Kemp, Robertson, and Jackson did so, and most of these contributors identified themselves as having

similarly extreme ideological positions. Clearly, some contributors are attracted to moderate candidates, and others support candidates who represent the
ideological wings of the parties. For some contributors, a label of extremely
liberal or extremely conservative is an attractive feature for a candidate, while
for others it is anathema.

That point is illustrated in the third column in Table 5.6. These data show
the average ideological distance between the contributor and the candidate to
whom he or she gave in 1988. Each entry represents the absolute value of
the distance between where the contributors placed themselves on the seven
point ideology scale, and where they placed the candidate to whom they
gave. Note that these distances are generally rather small, but that within
each party they are smaller for the candidates from the ideological wing of
that party. This strongly suggests that contributors give to these extreme
candidates *because* of their ideology – and that ideological extremism is an
important candidate resource when it comes to raising money.

The distances are also significantly higher for those Democratic candidates who attracted Republican contributors and others motivated by material
goals through national and in-state personal networks. The average distance
between contributor and candidate is highest for Dukakis. Interestingly, the
average Dukakis contributor placed him- or herself closer to Dukakis's more
conservative running mate, Lloyd Bentsen, than to Dukakis himself. In addition, the average Simon contributor was closer to Dukakis in ideology than
was the average Dukakis contributor.[16]

The results discussed in this section consistently identify the three most
extreme candidates: Robertson, Jackson, and Kemp. For each of these
three candidates, a majority of their contributors were solicited through
direct mail as shown in Figure 4.1. This contrasts with a range of 15% to
28% among the other candidates. Simon, who is the fourth most extreme
candidate, raised 28% impersonally and is at the high end of this range.
His low percentage must be considered somewhat of an anomaly if we try
to explain our findings simply on the basis of ideological extremism.
Simon, however, had more resources (most notably congressional office)
to build networks than did the other extreme candidates. Robertson and
Jackson lacked any resource associated with elective office, and Kemp as a
House Republican had less access to the congressional policy agenda than
did Simon as a Senate Democrat.[17] Thus our results overall strongly support the argument that ideological extremism is a potent resource for
impersonal solicitation, but it is not a resource that is useful in building
national networks of personal solicitation.

Are contributors ideologically extreme?

When candidates seek to position themselves to attract campaign money, they must consider the general ideology of the contributing pool. It has become accepted wisdom in political science that political activists in both parties are more attentive to ideological concerns and are more ideologically extreme than the general public. Newspapers routinely report polls of convention delegates showing that they are more extreme than the general public, a finding that echoes scholarly research (Kirkpatrick 1976; Rapoport, Abramowitz, and McGlennon 1986).

Some have also argued that primary election voters are more ideologically extreme than the general electorate, and have credited these extreme voters with eliminating moderate candidates who might have a chance of both winning and governing effectively (Lengle 1981; Polsby 1983; Walker 1988). Candidates presumably are drawn away from the ideological center in the search for primary votes, which later hurts them in the general election. There is some debate about the ideological representativeness of primary voters (see Norrander 1989), but there seems to be a consensus that party *activists* hold more extreme ideological positions than the general public.

It seems possible, therefore, that those who contribute to candidates may also be more ideologically extreme. This has important implications. If candidates must seek contributions from donors with extreme views on policy matters, they may adopt noncentrist positions in order to gather funds. Moreover, if the contributor pool is more extreme than the general public, extreme candidates may be relatively advantaged by the money they can collect from these individuals, and extremism may be a more valuable resource than moderation. To determine if contributors are more extreme than party supporters, we compare the responses of our contributors in 1988 with those of respondents to the 1988 NES. We have selected NES respondents who identified with each party and who reported voting in the general and primary elections.

Of course, the members of the contributor pool who choose to give in a particular election, and the new entrants to that pool, are partly a function of the candidates running. Had Robertson not campaigned in 1988, it is likely that a number of the conservative evangelical contributors to his campaign might have sat out the campaign, and the Republican contributors would have therefore been somewhat more moderate. Many of Robertson's contributors did sit out the campaign in 1992, despite the campaign of conservative Republican Pat Buchanan.[18] Yet it is also true that candidates such as Robertson can run because of the existence of ideologically proximate con-

Table 5.7. *The ideological representativeness of contributors*

	General–election voters	Primary voters	Contributors (all)	Contributors (party)
Republicans				
Defense spending	4.39	4.45	4.09	4.15
Detente	3.91	4.22	4.22	4.27
Guaranteed job	5.14	5.20	5.41	5.48
Minority aid	4.87	4.97	4.62	4.67
Women's role	2.68	2.95	2.94	2.97
Democrats				
Defense spending	3.47	3.60	2.69	2.34
Detente	3.62	3.71	2.68	2.41
Guaranteed job	4.03	4.06	3.66	3.19
Minority aid	4.06	4.10	3.09	2.64
Women's role	2.51	2.49	1.84	1.64

Mean scores are on 7-point items for each group.

tributors in the pool, and not only because they are able to add new members to the set of individuals who have given in the past.

In Table 5.7, we compare the ideological positions of our contributors with those of primary and general election voters who identified with the party of the candidate to whom they contributed. We present first the average position of all contributors to candidates within a party, and then the average position of contributors who gave to candidates within that party and who shared the partisanship of the candidate to whom they gave. On every issue those who gave to Democratic candidates were more liberal than both general-election and primary voters, and this was especially true for Democratic partisans. In contrast, Republican contributors were more extreme than primary voters on only one issue – job guarantees – and were noticeably more moderate on defense spending and minority aid. Republican contributors who are Republican partisans were more extreme than Republican primary voters on only two items. The data in Table 5.7 provide some tentative evidence that the search for individual contributions may pull candidates toward more extreme ideological positions in the Democratic party, but not in the Republican party. In the latter, contributors are not consistently more conservative than primary election voters, and they are actually more moderate than general-election voters on some issues.

Of course, our study of serious money does not include a full sample of contributors of small amounts. Those who gave small amounts in response to direct mail solicitations by Robertson, Kemp, Jackson, and Simon may have been even more extreme than those who gave sizable gifts to these candidates. Because we sampled contributors who had *aggregated* gifts of $200 or more, however, we did survey a number of contributors who made several small gifts that eventually totaled $200 or more. Over 20% of those who gave to Dole and Jackson, more than 33% of those who gave to Simon, more than 40% of those who gave to Kemp, and more than half of Robertson's contributors made such contributions of less than $200. We can therefore empirically investigate the ideological differences between those who made small and larger contributions to these candidates.[19]

We constructed three scales that measured attitudes on social issues, economic issues, and foreign and defense issues.[20] In addition, most of the contributors received a version of the questionnaire that contained a list of policy proposals designed to make America more competitive abroad. From this last set of items, we constructed three scales that measure support for a national industrial policy, regulatory and tax relief for business, and protectionism.

Our analysis suggests that those who made small donations were somewhat more ideologically extreme than those who made larger gifts, but the differences were generally small. We are most confident of our estimates for Robertson: his contributors were oversampled in this study, so our data contain a sizable number of donors who made small and large gifts to his campaign. We correlated the issue scales with the size of the contribution and found that the relationships were quite small and not statistically significant. For Jackson, Simon, Kemp, and Dole the correlations were occasionally larger (reaching .25 in a few instances), but because they had fewer contributors of small gifts the relationships rarely achieved statistical significance. Taken together, these data suggest that contributors who make small donations may be marginally more ideologically extreme but do not differ markedly in their ideological views from those who make larger gifts to the same candidates.

We compared the ideology of the contributors to those in the NES mass sample to explore the degree to which contributors' beliefs are consistent. Converse (1964) suggested that some individuals have belief systems in which the separate opinions are generally congruent with each other, but that most citizens hold inconsistent beliefs. Converse discussed the sources of this attitude constraint, and much subsequent research has been focused on measuring and debating the level of constraint in the general public. There are two general types of constraint. Horizontal constraint refers to the correlations among specific issue positions; for example, between attitudes toward affirmative action for blacks on the one hand and abortion on the other. Vertical constraint is the association between abstract ideological positions or values and concrete issue positions: for example, between liberalism per se and support for government programs to help the poor.

Brown et al. (1980b) found that contributors to presidential campaigns in 1972 showed higher levels of horizontal constraint than the general electorate. Our analysis of the 1988 data also shows highly constrained belief systems among campaign contributors. Across the five issues that were common to our survey and to the NES, the average interitem gamma correlation for the general public was .17, and for the contributors it was .48. A similar level of horizontal constraint was evident on other issue items in the survey. Vertical constraint was also high among contributors. The average gamma correlation between general ideology and the specific issue positions listed in Table 5.6 was .60, compared with .24 for the general public. Finally, contributors showed a high degree of dynamic constraint as well. The correlation between abstract ideology in 1988 and 1992 was .88, and nearly six in ten were perfectly stable in their ideological self-placement between the two surveys. In contrast, in the shorter 1990-92 NES panel, the correlation between ideology *for those who could place themselves on this scale* was .62.

Ideological constituencies

Exploiting ideological proximity as a resource is not a trivial exercise. Campaigns must identify and target those for whom ideological proximity is important – and such people certainly do not constitute the entire universe of potential contributors. Furthermore, to the extent campaigns can position their candidates, they must take into consideration what Kessel (1980) calls the structure of the competition. They must base their calculations on where the money is located and how stiff the competition is for that money at each location.

We examine the role of ideological proximity in more detail throughout the rest of this chapter, looking at the differences between those for whom proximity is important and those for whom it is not, as well as the ideological constellations of contributors and candidates within each party.

The sizable number of Republican contributors to most of the Democratic candidates did not share the candidate's ideological views and also differed sharply from other contributors to the candidate in their ideology. In addition, some contributors who shared the partisanship of the candidate they gave to contributed primarily because of nonideological resources the candidate controlled, especially the material benefits distributed by in-state networks. This suggests that to examine fully the role of ideology as a resource, we must first identify those contributors who are attracted to candidates because of their policy views, and distinguish them from those who contribute for other reasons. Those contributors who give to a campaign because of the political positions of the candidate constitute what might be called the ideological constituency for that candidate. We cannot identify those individuals who gave exclusively or predominately because of ideology. However, we can identify a subset of the sample in which these individuals are more likely to be found. We operationally define a candidate's ideological constituency as those contributors who have positive scores on our purposive motivation scale – that is, they are above the mean on purposive motives. Our data show that those high on purposive motives are far more likely than other contributors to contribute to the candidate who is closer to their own position than any other candidate still in the race. Indeed, when we estimated a logistic regression equation with this measure of ideological proximity to the candidate as the dependent variable and the three motives as independent variables, purposive motives were by far the strongest predictor.[21]

However, even when we isolated those who were especially high on purposive motives, it was still true that more than one in eight contributors to Democratic candidates were Republicans who did not share the ideology of the candidate. Closer analysis reveals that in every case, these Republican contributors were also high on material motives, and each contributor also gave to at least one Republican candidate to whom he or she was more ideologically proximate. These data suggest that the contribution to the Democratic candidate was made primarily for material reasons. We therefore add an element to our operational definition of ideological constituency: we count those contributors who gave to candidates of both parties in the ideological constituency of the party to which they are most ideologically proximate.

In Table 5.8, we show the importance of the concept of ideological constituency. We have identified contributors who are a part of the ideological constituency of each candidate, and those who are not. We then show the percentage of contributors in each group for whom the candidate to which they gave was ideologically as proximate as any other still in the race. The data show that a substantial portion of contributors in the ideological constituency of each candidate were contributing to the candidate who most closely shared their ideological views.

Table 5.8. *Ideological proximity to candidates among
ideological constituencies and other contributors*

	Ideological constituency, %	Other contributors, %
Bush	62	69
Dole	49	57
du Pont	50	50
Kemp	62	63
Robertson	76	74
Babbitt	74	52
Dukakis	59	42
Gephardt	75	29
Gore	64	27
Jackson	83	68
Simon	49	47

We show the percentage of contributors for whom the candidate
they supported financially was ideologically as proximate as any
other still in the race. The 7-point liberalism-conservatism scale is
the basis of comparison.

Among Republicans, there was little difference between the ideological
constituency of a candidate and the rest of the contributors, who were not
attracted by ideology. Most contributors who were especially motivated by
material concerns were Republican, and Republican candidates were therefore more likely to share their political views. Among Democrats, there was a
sharp division between contributors who were part of the candidate's ideological constituency and those who were not. For Babbitt, Dukakis, Gephardt,
and Gore, the effect was primarily due to the removal of Republicans who
gave to the campaigns for material motives, and also, in the case of Dukakis,
to the removal of in-state contributors who were motivated by material goals.
For Jackson, the effect is primarily a racial one, for whites were more likely
to be a part of Jackson's ideological constituency as defined by the purposive
motivation than were his black contributors.

Members of Simon's ideological constituency, however, were not noticeably more likely than his other contributors to have given to their ideologically
closest candidate, and Simon had the smallest percentage of contributors for
whom he was the closest candidate. Those solicited by mail were the most
likely to share Simon's political views: fully 71% of those who gave to Simon

in response to direct mail solicitation were closest to his ideological position. Interestingly, members of Simon's ideological constituency who were ideologically closer to a different candidate were almost evenly divided between strong liberals who were closer to Jackson, but may have contributed to Simon because he was more electable in their view, and more moderate, generally in-state Democrats who were closer to Gephardt and Gore but who may have contributed to Simon because he was the hometown candidate.

Throughout the rest of this section we distinguish between those contributors who are part of a candidate's ideological constituency and those who are not. As we will see, the differences between these two groups are substantively important.

Issue groups within the parties

Kessel (1980) has argued that presidential candidates must assemble their coalitions from preexisting issue groups of activists in each party. He identified five Republican issue groups and seven groups among Democrats, which he suggested represent relatively enduring cleavages within the parties. Green and Guth (1984; 1988) have suggested that similar cleavages exist within the ranks of political contributors, and such blocs constitute important fault lines among party elites.

If such party cleavages exist, we should see them in the ideological differences among those who gave to different candidates. We present the issue positions of those who gave to the 1988 candidates in Table 5.9.[22] For each candidate, we first show the issue positions of contributors who are part of the candidate's ideological constituency, and then the issue positions of those who are not. Although Table 5.9 shows only the data for the summary scales described above, we have also examined each separate opinion item and report those results when they differ from the overall pattern.

The data in Table 5.9 suggest that the most important ideological division among the ideological constituencies of Republican candidates in 1988 was between those who gave to Pat Robertson and those who gave to other candidates. Robertson's contributors were the most conservative of all Republican contributors on every issue except regulatory and tax relief for business and industrial policy, and they were significantly more likely than contributors to any other Republican to favor trade barriers. Perhaps even more remarkably, they were significantly more conservative on these scales than those who gave to Jack Kemp. Robertson's contributors were even more conservative than those who gave to Kemp on the gold standard, an

Table 5.9. *Issue positions of candidate ideological constituencies*

	Bush	Dole	du Pont	Kemp	Robertson
Ideological Constituency					
Social issues	.20	.05	-.03	.42	.96
Economic issues	.31	.22	.24	.53	.69
Foreign policy	.36	.31	.36	.64	.87
Industrial policy	.16	.15	.49	.21	.40
Tax/regulation relief	.29	.34	.32	.61	.31
Protectionism	.09	.15	.50	-.09	-.32
Other Contributors					
Social issues	.00	.06	-.09	.19	.82
Economic issues	.02	.16	.05	.45	.58
Foreign policy	.11	.27	-.17	.48	.68
Industrial policy	.15	.12	.10	.11	.08
Tax/regulation relief	.23	.13	.15	.45	.27
Protectionism	.18	.09	.18	.04	-.40

	Babbitt	Dukakis	Gephardt	Gore	Jackson	Simon
Ideological Constituency						
Social issues	-.71	-.65	-.30	-.57	-.75	-.82
Economic issues	-.90	-.81	-.85	-.46	-1.10	-.98
Foreign policy	-.89	-.76	-.79	-.63	-1.11	-.98
Industrial policy	-.38	-.37	-.43	-.30	-.43	-.16
Tax/regulation relief	-.80	-.61	-.57	-.24	-.76	-.85
Protectionism	-.01	-.01	-.39	-.12	-.11	.26
Other Contributors						
Social issues	-.46	-.35	-.07	-.17	-.50	-.56
Economic issues	-.26	-.37	.00	-.12	-.74	-.66
Foreign policy	-.37	-.42	-.18	-.22	-.91	-.62
Industrial policy	.07	-.02	-.07	-.19	-.41	-.29
Tax/regulation relief	-.37	-.23	.12	-.05	-.58	-.52
Protectionism	.23	.07	.13	.07	.08	.13

Mean scores on scales for each group. The items used to construct each scale were normalized and then averaged to produce the scale.

issue emphasized only by the Kemp campaign. Those who gave to Kemp were, in turn, more conservative than those who gave to Bush, Dole, or du Pont on all items except industrial policy and protection, and so another division emerged between Kemp contributors and those to the three more moderate candidates.

Among those who gave to Democrats, those who gave to Simon and especially to Jackson were the most liberal, while those who gave to Gore and especially to Gephardt were more moderate. The contributors who gave to a Democratic candidate but who were not part of the candidate's ideological constituency were significantly more conservative than contributors who were part of that constituency. Note especially the large difference on economic issues between Gephardt and Gore contributors.

These results augment our earlier findings, which showed that contributors to Democratic candidates were more ideologically extreme than Democratic primary voters. Contributors who care about issues are even more extreme than Democratic contributors who are motivated by other concerns. Those who give because they are interested in policy concerns may be expected to exert a leftward pull beyond that of contributors generally. Candidates, after all, are probably most responsive in terms of their policy choices to contributors who are interested in policy choices.

The data in Table 5.9 also show that among ideological constituencies, economic issues sharply separate Republicans from Democrats. The exception is protectionism, which in 1988 split each party. Those who gave to Gephardt and especially Robertson were the most favorable toward protectionist measures, while those who gave to Bush, Dole, du Pont, and Simon were the most supportive of free trade. The other issues that showed potential for cross-party cleavages were social concerns. Those who gave to Bush, Dole, and du Pont, as well as to Gephardt and to some extent Gore, were relatively moderate on social issues. The abortion issue was the most obvious example: a majority of those who gave to every Republican candidate except Robertson opposed banning abortions.

In Table 5.10, we use a different set of measures to show the ideological divisions between candidate constituencies. We asked contributors to place themselves on a seven-point general liberal–conservative scale, and also to place themselves on similar scales based on their views on social issues, economic issues, and defense issues. The data in Table 5.10 show the mean self-placement on these scales for the contributors to each candidate. Once again we distinguish between contributors who were part of the candidate's ideological constituency and those who were not.

The pattern of these data is similar to that in Table 5.9, but from this table we can see how various blocs of contributors perceive their own ideological positions. The ideological constituencies of all candidates but Robertson perceived themselves to be relatively more liberal on social issues than on other issues, but those who gave to Robertson saw themselves as most conservative

Table 5.10. *Ideological self-placement of candidate ideological constituencies*

	Bush	Dole	du Pont	Kemp	Robertson	
Ideological Constituency						
Overall ideology	5.59	5.44	5.42	5.99	6.22	
Social issues	4.98	5.11	3.97	5.67	6.57	
Economic issues	5.78	5.90	5.75	6.09	6.22	
Defense policy	5.40	5.43	5.27	5.92	5.92	
Other Contributors						
Overall ideology	5.36	5.15	5.13	5.92	6.03	
Social issues	4.71	4.94	4.21	5.61	6.57	
Economic issues	5.49	5.60	5.31	6.01	6.05	
Defense policy	5.31	5.06	4.93	5.75	5.86	
	Babbitt	Dukakis	Gephardt	Gore	Jackson	Simon
Ideological Constituency						
Overall ideology	2.41	2.61	3.13	3.18	1.87	2.02
Social issues	2.00	2.32	2.88	2.59	2.01	1.97
Economic issues	2.92	2.93	3.26	3.33	2.12	2.43
Defense policy	2.42	2.71	3.40	3.29	2.31	2.09
Other Contributors						
Overall ideology	3.10	3.18	3.97	3.88	2.10	2.63
Social issues	2.58	2.73	3.61	3.32	2.19	4.32
Economic issues	3.62	3.56	4.18	4.08	2.33	3.06
Defense policy	3.27	3.32	4.18	3.32	2.49	2.68

Mean scores on four 7-point scales for each group. Overall ideology is based on the 7-point lib-eralism-conservatism scale.

on these matters. The moderation of most contributors on social issues is not surprising, for research has consistently shown that elites are more liberal on issues such as abortion and gay rights than is the mass public (Cook, Jelen, and Wilcox 1992; Sniderman, Brody, and Tetlock 1992). For nearly all candidates, the members of their ideological constituency saw themselves as most conservative on economic issues. This is also not surprising, given the substantial incomes of these contributors, described in Chapter 3.

Most Republican contributors who rated themselves as moderate on social issues and who took moderate positions on the concrete social issues but who took conservative positions on economic issues placed themselves as conservatives on the general ideology scale. In contrast, Democrats who took moderate positions on economic issues but liberal positions on social issues rated themselves as liberal. This suggests the possibility that for this select group, liberalism and conservatism might have different issue consequences. To test this possibility, we regressed general ideological self-placement on the six issue scales and also included interaction terms between these scales and partisanship. The results (not shown) indicated that economic issues were important sources of ideological self-placement for both Republican and Democratic contributors. Social issues were important only for Democrats, while support for tax and regulatory relief were significant only for Republicans. This suggests that Republican contributors base their ideological self-placement primarily on economic issues, while Democratic contributors consider both their economic and social issue positions.

There is consensus among Republican contributors of serious money for action on a conservative economic agenda. There is, however, a large pool of serious money contributors in the Republican party whose members do not support action on the conservative social agenda. In the Democratic party, by contrast, there is more consensus among the ideological constituency on both social and economic agendas.

One final point is evident from these data. Although the candidates sometimes took carefully nuanced positions on issues in a given domain, the contributors to each candidate for the most part order themselves similarly on most issues. Robertson's and Kemp's contributors were more conservative than those who gave to Bush, Dole, and du Pont on all issues in the survey, except protectionism, which does not fit neatly into a left–right ordering. Among the Democrats, those who gave to Jackson and Simon were the most liberal on economic and foreign policy issues, while those who gave to Gore and Gephardt were the most conservative on nearly every issue in the survey. The exception for the Democrats is the relatively moderate positions of Simon's and especially Jackson's contributors on social and cultural issues. Jackson's black contributors were more moderate than the whites who contributed to his campaign. Despite a modest number of cases, we can conclude that black contributors to Jackson were significantly more moderate than whites on each of the six issue scales except industrial policy.

Ideology as group affect

Conover and Feldman (1981) have argued that ideological identification is as much a function of affect toward social and political groups as of policy preferences. Individuals may use affective responses to social groups in sorting out their responses to candidates and parties. Sniderman, Brody, and

Tetlock (1991) suggest that individuals use a "likability heuristic" toward social and political groups in determining their ideological responses and their reactions to policies. They argue that polar affect toward social groups on both sides of the political divide – for example, liberals and conservatives, the Moral Majority, and the American Civil Liberties Union (ACLU) – is actually more important in influencing the policy views of political sophisticates than those with little political information. It may be useful, therefore, to consider affect toward opposing sets of political and social groups as yet another measure of political ideology.

In Table 5.11, we show the affect of contributors to various candidates toward a number of opposing social and political groups and institutions. The entries are feeling thermometer scores, which asked respondents to rate each group on a scale ranging from 0 to 100, where 50 was neutral; scores above 50 indicate the degree of "warmth" the respondent felt toward the group, and scores below 50 the degree of "coldness."[23] Once again, we first present the data for contributors from the ideological constituency of each candidate, then show similar figures for others who gave to the candidate.

The data provide additional evidence for the split between Robertson's Republicans and others who gave to candidates in that party. The contributors in Robertson's ideological constituency were the only set to rate the Moral Majority warmly, and they also rated the NRA and conservatives relatively more warmly than did contributors to any other Republican. They rated the ACLU, liberals, and feminists very coolly – more so than contributors to any other Republican, although they were slightly warmer toward labor unions than were donors to some other Republicans. It is also interesting to note that although in general Democrats rated the Supreme Court more coolly than did Republicans, Robertson's contributors were the most negative toward the Court of any in either party. On the "700 Club," Robertson continues to deride the "liberal Court," and his contributors appear to agree with his assessment.[24]

Among all Democratic contributors, those who gave to Jackson and Simon showed more polar affect toward ideological groups, while those who gave to Gephardt and especially Gore showed less polarization in their evaluations of these groups. Once again, contributors to Democrats who were not part of a candidate's ideological constituencies were much more conservative. For Babbitt, Dukakis, Gephardt, and Gore, contributors who were not attracted by ideology rated big business more warmly than labor unions, and those who gave to Gephardt and especially Gore rated conservatives more warmly than liberals.

Table 5.11. *Feeling thermometer scores for social and political groups*

	Bush	Dole	du Pont	Kemp	Robertson
Ideological Constituency					
Moral Majority	36	31	15	48	77
NRA	46	45	31	51	56
Feminists	28	30	27	19	6
ACLU	22	31	24	21	4
Civil rights leaders	33	33	33	28	30
Big business	61	63	50	56	55
Labor unions	24	23	25	33	28
Conservatives	71	75	61	79	87
Liberals	21	21	28	16	11
Supreme Court	73	75	69	65	51
Other Contributors					
Moral Majority	29	36	20	32	68
NRA	36	31	25	32	45
Feminists	36	36	35	21	11
ACLU	29	34	26	19	8
Civil rights leaders	38	39	40	31	28
Big business	63	61	54	53	49
Labor unions	33	31	31	23	27
Conservatives	64	66	56	69	80
Liberals	29	30	30	20	12
Supreme Court	74	72	69	68	53

	Babbitt	Dukakis	Gephardt	Gore	Jackson	Simon
Ideological Constituency						
Moral Majority	7	15	9	8	7	6
NRA	10	8	8	9	4	6
Feminists	61	64	52	54	70	66
ACLU	63	65	53	53	73	71
Civil rights leaders	69	71	60	59	81	73
Big business	40	42	42	41	37	35
Labor unions	58	53	56	42	64	63
Conservatives	24	30	31	31	25	23
Liberals	74	69	58	53	74	75
Supreme Court	54	61	57	65	57	61
Other Contributors						
Moral Majority	14	14	23	24	9	11
NRA	23	20	25	34	12	13
Feminists	53	46	37	41	61	59
ACLU	59	52	33	39	65	60
Civil rights leaders	54	52	40	45	76	66
Big business	50	46	54	55	40	46
Labor unions	44	43	31	36	56	52
Conservatives	45	37	49	55	33	35
Liberals	54	49	36	36	67	60
Supreme Court	68	64	65	60	53	61

More generally, the cool reaction by both Republican and Democratic contributors to groups representing the social right is striking. Only those who gave to Robertson were warm toward the Moral Majority and the NRA, while contributors to Bush, Dole, du Pont, and most Democrats were quite cool, and Kemp's contributors were neutral. The generally cool response of Democratic ideological constituencies to organized labor is also notable: the contributors for every candidate rated labor more coolly than the ACLU, feminists, and civil rights leaders.

This result may be taken as a commentary on the declining role of organized labor in the Democratic nomination process. To the extent that campaign contributions have influence over candidates, it is highly probable that their priorities lie with the interests of groups other than labor. This should not be entirely surprising, given that Democratic contributors of serious money are predominantly professionals, but these results do illustrate the extent to which organized labor fails to command the affections of these key players in the nomination process. Labor leaders say that union members and union officials generally do not contribute directly to candidates. Instead most labor money in recent years has come to candidates through PACs (Wilcox 1994). PACs, however, play a minor role in presidential nomination finance – and labor, therefore is not generally a major player in the funding of presidential nomination candidates.[25]

Overall, Republicans were quite cool toward labor unions and warm toward business, while Democratic contributors were more neutral toward each. Democrats were quite cool toward the symbols of the cultural right and warm toward those of the left, while Republican contributors, with the exception of those who gave to Robertson, were cool toward each. Thus Republican contributors responded more strongly to the symbols of the New Deal alignment, while Democratic contributors appeared to respond more strongly to the symbols of the new cultural politics.

Multivariate analysis

To sort out the role of issues and group affect in determining each candidate's ideological constituency, we performed two separate discriminant analyses, with candidate choice as the dependent variable. The independent variables were the six issue scales, and measures of affect toward pairs of social groups.[26] Once again we do not present the results in tabular form, but we will summarize them.

The analysis for Democratic candidates revealed that the most fundamental division among candidates' ideological constituencies was a basic left-right split. The first function distinguished between those who gave to the candidates on the left (Jackson and Simon), candidates in the center (Babbitt and Dukakis), and candidates on the right of the Democratic party (Gephardt and Gore). This function explained more than two-thirds of the variance. A second function identified the protectionism split among the Democratic candidates, distinguishing between those who gave to Jackson and Gephardt on the one hand, and to Babbitt and Simon on the other.

The analysis for Republicans revealed that the candidacy of Robertson exacerbated the deep divisions within the party. The first function explained fully 75% of the variance, and it distinguished those who gave to Robertson from those who gave to any other Republican candidate. Robertson's contributors were distinctive in their conservatism on most policy issues, their warm affect toward the social right, their antipathy for the social left, and their protectionist sentiments. A second function divided those who gave to du Pont and Kemp from those who gave to other Republican candidates. Du Pont's and Kemp's ideological constituencies were distinctive in their support for tax and regulatory relief to help business deal with foreign competition, and in their conservative positions on economic policy, after holding constant their views on other issues.

It is also interesting to note that although the discriminant analysis did quite well in predicting support for most candidates, it was less successful in predicting contributions to Bush, Dukakis, and Babbitt. For each of the other candidates, the analysis correctly predicted nearly half of their ideological constituency, but for these three candidates, only one in four contributors was correctly identified. We suspect that these results reflect the very short duration of the Babbitt campaign, which never moved beyond attracting seed money, and the fact that Bush and Dukakis won their party's nomination and therefore attracted to their campaign contributors with a wider array of ideological positions.

The deep divide between Robertson's constituency and those of other Republican candidates is evident in analysis of feeling thermometers toward the candidates. Those who gave to other Republican candidates were generally hostile toward Robertson's candidacy: between 10% and 20% of contributors to the other Republican candidates rated Robertson at 0°, the most negative possible score. Fully a third of Bush's contributors and nearly half of those who gave to du Pont rated Robertson less favorably than they rated Dukakis. Even among Kemp's contributors, a sizable minority preferred Dukakis to Robertson. Nearly a third of those who gave to the three moderate Republican candidates rated Jesse Jackson higher than Robertson.

Candidate resources and ideological coalitions

Although candidate ideological constituencies may be narrow, the other resources discussed above allow candidates to draw from contributors with a somewhat wider range of positions. In the top half of Table 5.12 we show in a somewhat different manner the role of ideology in candidate coalitions. Table 5.12 shows all contributors to the candidates, not just those we have defined as a part of the ideological constituency of a candidate. We have ordered the candidates from left to right based on the placement of the candidates by contributors in their party, shown in Table 5.5. The entries in the top half of Table 5.12 are the percentage of all contributors to a candidate who placed themselves at each location on a seven-point liberal–conservative scale, which shows the distribution of a candidate's ideological support. For example, 40% of those who gave to Jackson rated themselves as extremely liberal, but 6% called themselves slightly conservative. For ease of presentation, we do not show cells with fewer than 5% of a candidate's contributors.

The data show that Democratic candidates attracted a fairly sizable number of conservative contributors, but that few liberals gave to Republican candidates. Most candidates were able to attract contributions from individuals with a fairly wide range of ideological positions, but Kemp and especially Robertson had a more narrow ideological base. Although Jackson had the highest percentage of contributors who placed themselves at the extreme end of the ideological spectrum, he also attracted a number of moderate and even slightly conservative contributors, principally among his black constituency.

In the bottom half of Table 5.12, we show the same data from a different angle. The entries in this section represent the percentage of those with each ideological position who gave to each candidate. For example, 56% of extremely liberal contributors gave to Jackson, while 5% gave to Gore. To ease presentation, we do not show cells with fewer than 5% of contributors. These data show that Jackson and Robertson each corralled more than half of the contributors who took extreme ideological positions, and Dukakis received gifts from more than half of the liberals. Those who called themselves slightly liberal, moderate, or slightly conservative split their money more widely, with many candidates receiving a share of the contributions of these groups. Conservatives divided their money between Bush and Robertson, and to a lesser extent Dole and Kemp. It is interesting to see the breadth of the appeal of Dukakis and Bush, who received a significant share of contributions from individuals with a wide range of ideological positions. Many contributors clearly gave to candidates for reasons other than ideology, including especially the material and solidary motives that are activated in national and in-state networks.

Table 5.12. *The ideology of candidate constituencies*

| | Extremely liberal | | | | | | Extremely conservative |
	1	2	3	4	5	6	7
Composition of Candidate Coalitions[a], %							
Jackson	40	33	16	6	6		
Simon	12	44	19	12	7	6	
Dukakis		48	19	11	14	6	
Babbitt	6	33	28	21	7	5	
Gore		24	27	12	20	16	
Gephardt		21	24	19	23	13	
Dole			5	19	34	31	5
du Pont			10	13	25	38	7
Bush				6	34	51	5
Kemp					12	67	16
Robertson					7	64	25

| | Extremely liberal | | | | | | Extremely conservative |
	1	2	3	4	5	6	7
Contributors Decisions on Candidate Preference[b], %							
Jackson	56	6	6				
Simon	22	11	8	5			
Dukakis		56	33	24	15		
Babbitt	7	5	7	6			
Gore	5	11	19	11	9		
Gephardt			12	12	7		
Dole			5	19	19	13	
du Pont				7	5	6	
Bush			7	10	33	31	20
Kemp						14	19
Robertson					5	25	53
n	38	215	140	118	234	376	68

[a]Each cell is the percent of a candidate's contributors at that scale value on liberalism-conservatism.
[b]Each cell is the percent of all contributors at that scale value on liberalism-conservatism who were sampled as contributing to that candidate.
For purposes of presentation, only cells with at least 5% are shown.

Kessel (1980) argued that the structure of the competition influences the outcome of presidential prenomination candidates, as several candidates vie for different blocs of party voters. These data suggest that in the structure of financial competition in 1988, Jackson and Simon competed for the contributions of the extremely liberal members of the pool; Babbitt, Dukakis, and Simon competed for liberals; and Dukakis, Gephardt, and Gore competed for those who were slightly liberal and for moderates. Among the Republicans, Bush, Dole, and to a lesser extent du Pont competed for the money of moderates and slightly conservative contributors, and Bush, Kemp, and Robertson competed for contributions from conservatives and extremely conservative donors.

Conclusions

Candidates differ in the resources that they can offer to potential contributors. Sitting governors and, to a lesser extent, senators and members of the House can offer material and solidary motives to in-state contributors, who serve as the nucleus of their early fundraising efforts. Candidates from large states are clearly advantaged in this resource, for those from smaller states can raise far less in-state money, even if their yield is high. Candidates can also assemble national networks. These networks are idiosyncratic, for they depend on the connections of individuals located at different levels of the pyramid. In 1988, these networks frequently relied on party activists, who were motivated by solidary goals, and on the material benefits that can be provided by congressional office. In addition, networks based on social identity were formed among Greek, Jewish, black, and charismatic Christian citizens.

Ideology is also a resource, and can be used by moderate and more extreme candidates. For extreme candidates, ideology can help raise large sums through small gifts that fall outside our study of serious money, yet our data suggest that these contributors have political views similar to those who make larger donations. Among those motivated by purposive goals, contributors generally give to candidates who share their ideological views.

Candidates must assess their own resources, then develop strategies to approach potential contributors. Those who try to build in-state or national networks also must identify and approach solicitors. Potential contributors and solicitors are approached by multiple candidates, and so must make a series of decisions about whom to support. These decisions are the focus of Chapter 6.

6. Recruiting contributors and solicitors: Candidate and individual decisions

We have shown that there exists a relatively constant pool of campaign contributors with a heterogeneous set of motives that are approached by candidates either through personal networks or through mail and telemarketing. Although campaigns often seek to expand the pool of contributors by attracting new members, two of the most basic decisions by campaign strategists are which segments of the existing pool to target and how to target them. Individual contributors must then decide whether or not to respond to a solicitation by a campaign. In addition, when campaigns employ personal networking, they must develop a strategy to identify which of their contributors will be asked to solicit others to give. Those asked to solicit must in turn decide whether or not to invest the time, energy, and social capital to do so.

Our panel study of 1988 and 1992 contributors enables us to examine these series of decisions by campaigns, contributors, and potential solicitors. The 1988 data consisted entirely of people who were asked to give and who gave, so we cannot compare them to those members of the pool who were not asked or who were asked but chose not to give in 1988. Thus, using the 1988 data alone we cannot examine campaign decisions about whom to solicit, or contributor decisions about whether to contribute. The 1992 survey asked the 1988 contributors whether they were asked to give in 1992, whether they gave, whether they were asked to solicit others to give, and whether they did solicit. The panel study therefore allows us to examine the decision calculus of candidates and potential contributors, which cross-sectional studies cannot do. Thus we can compare those who were asked to give with those who were not asked, those who gave in response to a request with those who refused, those who were asked to solicit with those who were not, and those who did solicit when asked with those who said no. Our panel survey therefore allows us to examine decisions by members of the pool to give in subsequent election cycles.[1]

Who is asked to contribute?

Almost 90% of the contributors from 1988 who responded to the 1992 survey were solicited by at least one of the presidential candidates in 1992. This provides striking evidence of the extent to which candidates solicit most members of the existing pool. In fact, many of the 1988 contributors were solicited in 1992 by more than one candidate. Over a third were solicited by more than one candidate using direct mail or telemarketing, and 14% were solicited by more than one candidate through personal networks. Many contributors were solicited by more than one method, either by the same candidate or by different candidates.

Nearly one contributor in three was solicited by at least one candidate from each party. Five percent were actually solicited by all seven candidates from both parties. Those who were asked by both Republican and Democratic candidates were disproportionately likely to express material motives and to be regular givers to all types of candidates and to party committees. Despite the fact that cross-party giving is found more often in personal networks, cross-party solicitations are more common through direct mail. This should not be surprising because, as noted in Chapter 4, candidates prospect group membership lists, magazine subscription lists, and other lists that may be expected to contain large numbers of contributors from both parties.

Overall, 43% of the contributors were *personally* solicited on behalf of at least one candidate, and 70% were *impersonally* solicited. In Table 6.1 we show that there is a relationship between the methods by which contributors were solicited in these two years. Those who were initially contacted in 1988 by either method were more likely than other contributors to be contacted by the same method in 1992.

In absolute terms, those first approached in 1988 by personal networks had a higher probability of being approached by mail than by a personal contact in 1992. Fully 70% of those who were initially solicited by personal networks in 1988 were asked to give to at least one candidate by direct mail or telemarketing in 1992, while only 52% were approached in person. It is easy for campaigns to mail solicitations to those who gave to other candidates in previous election cycles, including those initially solicited through personal networks. Once a contributor appears on such a list, impersonal contact is an obvious and easy means of approaching the prospect in the future.

The reverse is not true. Only 20% of those who were first solicited through impersonal means in 1988 received at least one personal-acquaintance solicitation in 1992. Those who appear on direct mail or telemarketing lists from

Table 6.1. *Continuity of method of solicitation: 1988–92*

	% Contacted personally at least once 1992	% Contacted impersonally at least once 1992
Contacted personally 1988	52	70
Contacted impersonally 1988	20	73

past campaigns are rarely solicited the next time through personal networks. To add a personal-acquaintance contributor to a mailing list is easy; to locate an acquaintance of someone on a mailing list who will be willing to approach that person is more difficult.

Who, then, was asked to contribute? The short answer is almost everyone, given that nearly 90% of 1988 contributors were asked again in 1992. In simple terms of being asked versus not being asked, there is little variance to explain. There is, however, considerable difference in how many campaigns solicited each individual. Some contributors were approached by one or two campaigns, others by most or all campaigns. We can calculate how many campaigns solicited contributions from each individual, and we can do this for the two principal methods of solicitation.

We described in Chapter 4 a strong relationship between motives and methods of successful solicitation. Of course, campaigns have no direct way of measuring the motivations of potential contributors. However, many solicitors working through personal networks have a good idea of what motivates their friends and business associates. Direct mail is, as we will see, less precisely targeted, but direct mail vendors do understand the motivational basis of contributing and have some knowledge of which populations may respond favorably to the incentives they have to offer. Thus, we would expect to find a relationship between contributors' motivations in 1988 and both the methods and frequency of solicitation in 1992. We expect that contributors who are higher on solidary and material motives will receive more campaign solicitations through personal networks than those who are lower, while contributors higher on purposive motives will be solicited by more campaigns using direct mail and telemarketing than those who are lower.

Table 6.2 shows the results of four regression analyses, each predicting the number of campaigns that solicited each contributor. The first column shows results for solicitations by personal networks, and the second for direct mail

Table 6.2. *OLS regression predicting how many 1992 candidates solicited the respondent*

	Solicited impersonally		Solicited personally	
	b	se	b	se
Basic model				
Purposive	.20	.07[b]	-.03	.05
Solidary	.21	.07[b]	.14	.05[b]
Material	-.08	.07	.13	.05[b]
Constant	1.48	.07	.68	.05
n	545		545	
Expanded model				
Purposive	.21	.08[b]	-.05	.06
Solidary	.06	.08	.08	.06
Material	-.18	.08[a]	.06	.06
1988 impersonal solicitation	-.08	.19	-.50	.13[b]
Index of campaign giving	.33	.10[b]	.05	.07
Index of campaign work	.02	.11	.09	.07
Income	-.01	.08	.09	.05[a]
Party official	.41	.22[a]	.11	.15
PAC contributing	.01	.07	.10	.05[a]
Jewish	.59	.22[a]	.33	.15[a]
Greek Orthodox	.59	.49	.55	.34[a]
Ideological extremism	.19	.10[a]	.05	.07
Constant	.97	.98	.93	.68
n	385		384	

[a]Significant at .05 in a one-tail test.
[b]Significant at .01 in a one-tail test.

and telemarketing.[2] The top of the table presents results from equations that include only measures of the three motives as independent variables. The results confirm our expectations. Those contributors who were higher on solidary and material motives in 1988 were solicited by more candidates in 1992 through personal networks than those who were lower on these motives. Those contributors who were higher on purposive motives in 1988 were solicited in 1992 by more candidates who used direct mail and telemarketing than those who were lower, and those who were higher on material motives were approached by fewer campaigns through these impersonal methods than those who were lower.

Somewhat surprisingly, we find that those who were higher on solidary motives in 1988 also were solicited by more candidates in 1992 who used impersonal methods than were those lower on such motives. It seems likely that those who join organizations because they are motivated by solidary concerns appear more frequently on membership lists of organizations, including party organizations, to which candidates routinely mail. With perhaps this exception, the campaigns therefore succeeded in soliciting contributors by a method appropriate to their basic motivations.

We can gain more insight into the targeting decisions of campaigns by examining some of the specific means by which individuals with particular motives can be identified. It seems likely that campaigns identify those to solicit through the mail by renting lists, so we include our measure of the Index of Campaign Giving and the Index of Campaign Work because individuals who frequently give to or work in campaigns are likely to appear on many mailing lists. It seems likely that campaigns identify those to solicit through networks by activating preexisting networks, so we also include a measure of the method by which the contributor was initially solicited in 1988. It also seems likely that personal networks develop more extensively among the wealthy, so we include a measure of personal income.

Because of the continuity of the candidate resources discussed in Chapter 5, campaigns have over the years developed methods for identifying those who are attracted to those resources. Both these methods and the lists produced by them are transferable to other campaigns. Some of these lists are found in the computers of direct mail specialists, and others are found on the Rolodexes of personal-network fundraisers who can be enlisted by a candidate. We include measures that identify contributors who are likely to respond to four of the candidate resources discussed in the previous chapter. We do not include a measure of a home-state base, because those who were in the home state of a 1988 candidate were not likely to be especially mobilized by 1992 candidates. To tap party and congressional networks we included measures of whether the individual was a party official, and how often he or she gave to PACs. To identify those in the social identity networks who were most likely to be mobilized in 1992, we included dichotomous variables to identify those with Jewish or Greek social identities. To tap the ideological resource, we included a measure of ideological extremism.

The results, shown at the bottom of Table 6.2, suggest that those individuals who are high on purposive motives and those who are low on material motives are more likely to be solicited through direct mail or telemarketing. Those who appear on lists of regular political contributors, of party officials, or of contributors to Jewish causes, or on lists that include individuals with extreme political views, receive more candidate solicitations through the mail.

The motives do not predict solicitation through personal networks after controlling for these resource lists. Those who had been solicited in 1988 through a personal network were much more likely to be asked again in this fashion in 1992, as were those who gave frequently to PACs, and those with Jewish or Greek social identities. Finally, affluent respondents were more likely to be solicited in networks than their less wealthy counterparts.

We have emphasized that these methods basically reach different kinds of people. This conclusion is borne out by these results because only one group, Jewish contributors, is solicited by both methods. We argue in Chapter 5 that the resources of party, congressional office, and social identity are best mobilized through national networks of personal solicitation. The data bear out our argument for congressional networks and social identity, although party officials are more likely than other contributors to receive mail requests and are no more likely to be contacted through networks. The last may be so for two reasons. First, party lists are relatively easy to obtain and presumably get a relatively high response rate. Second, many of the party officials in our study may have been lower-level local officials, such as party committee persons who do not make the large contributions typically networked. We also argued that ideological extremism is best mobilized by mail, a result confirmed by our data.

Who is solicited by whom?

Because we can identify which candidates in 1992 solicited the contributors to each candidate in 1988, we can make longitudinal comparisons between contributing patterns in 1988 and solicitation patterns in 1992. Because of small sample sizes in the 1992 study, however, we must be cautious when discussing subsets of contributors.

Perhaps the most remarkable result from this analysis is the extensive soliciting done by the Bush organization. His campaign solicited 80% or more of contributors to each of the 1988 Republican candidates, including Kemp and Robertson. He solicited 45% or more of the contributors to all of the 1988 Democratic candidates except Jackson and Simon.[3] Clinton also solicited widely, tapping nearly two-thirds of those who contributed to each of the 1988 Democratic candidates, and roughly one in four of those who contributed to the moderate Republicans Bush, Dole, and du Pont.

Other candidates were more selective. Buchanan solicited much more often from the constituency of Kemp and Robertson than from other candidates in 1988, although Bush solicited more than Buchanan did from both lists. Harkin solicited more of Simon's contributors than those who gave to other candidates, and Tsongas, who shared both a home-state residence and Greek ethnicity with Dukakis, solicited over half of Dukakis's contributors.

It may seem unusual that Bush solicited so heavily from the contributors of Democratic candidates in 1988. As shown in Chapter 5, however, a substantial number of those sampled as giving to Democrats identified and voted as Republicans. The Bush campaign solicited 74% of these Republicans who gave to Democratic candidates. Yet Bush also solicited an impressive 39% of all contributors who identified as Democrats, whom we sampled as contributing to a Democrat in 1988, and who reported voting for Dukakis in the general election. This result illustrates the remarkable diversity of the Bush campaign solicitation effort.

We estimated logistic regression equations to determine what special types of 1988 contributors were solicited by each candidate in 1992, after controlling for the 1988 candidate constituencies. Clinton more frequently solicited men, regular PAC contributors, Jewish contributors, and those who perceived themselves to be proximate to his ideological position. The disproportionate solicitation of the latter group confirms his use of Democratic Leadership Council contributor lists. Buchanan also targeted those proximate to his ideology. In 1992 Bush, despite presidential incumbency and a very broad-based effort, solicited 1988 contributors from Texas at a higher rate than he solicited 1988 donors from other states. Kerrey and Harkin reached regular party donors more often than other contributors in the 1988 pool. Tsongas solicited Greek Orthodox and Jewish contributors disproportionately, as well as those from Massachusetts.

The decision to contribute

Contributors must decide whether to respond to the solicitations from the various candidates who ask for their money. Although almost 90% of those we surveyed in 1992 were asked by at least one candidate to give, only 63% of all 1988 contributors actually gave. The 1992 data allow us to determine which of those members of the contributing pool who were asked to contribute actually did so. Sixty-nine percent of those who were solicited through a personal net-work gave contributions to one or more candidates, compared to 33% of those who were solicited impersonally.

In this section, we will measure contribution decisions in two distinct ways. Because contributions are made in response to solicitations, we will include in both analyses only those who were solicited by at least one candidate. First, we will determine who gave to one or more presidential candidates in 1992. That is, we look at who decided to give to any candidate in 1992. Second, we examine the decision to contribute or not contribute to each campaign that asked. To do this, one data set is constructed for each method of solicitation. Here the unit of analysis will be the campaign solicitation. For example, individuals who were solicited by three campaigns in the personal-solicitation data set will appear three times in this data set, with each case given one-third the weight for that individual. There is thus a separate record in the data set for each campaign that solicited that individual.

This second analysis will enable us to examine the role of candidate characteristics in the decision to contribute, especially the importance of the contributor's perception of ideological proximity to the candidate. Thus we can examine candidate factors in a way that is impossible if the question is simply whether an individual gave in response to any of the candidates that solicited him or her.

Who gives?

We begin by asking which members of the 1988 contributor pool who were solicited in 1992 actually decided to give to at least one of the candidates who solicited them. We expect that the factors discussed in the previous three chapters will help explain who gave in 1992. Because we are predicting whether an individual gave to any candidate in 1992, we do not wish in this case to make separate predictions for each of the two basic methods of solicitation. Our focus in this analysis is on the relationship between contributor characteristics and the decision to give to any candidate at all.

We expect the motives will predict the decision to contribute, because the more highly motivated a person is to participate in politics, the more likely it is that person will respond to a solicitation. We also expect, however, that these relationships will be modest, because contributors with certain motives respond positively to some methods of solicitation and neutrally or negatively to others. For example, individuals who are motivated by material concerns should be more likely to give in personal networks but less likely to give through the mail, while those with purposive motives should be more likely to respond to impersonal solicitations than personal ones. When we combine these two methods into a single equation we will naturally find weak relationships.

We expect individuals with extreme ideological views to be slightly more likely than others to give in response to all solicitations. As we noted earlier, 70% of respondents received a mail solicitation, compared to 43% who were solicited personally. Politically extreme individuals are more likely to respond to the more numerous mail solicitations than are the less politically extreme, thus establishing a relationship between extremism and contributing.

We expect that the more solicitations a potential contributor receives, the more likely that individual is to give. This should be especially true for personal solicitations, which, because of their rich reward structure, have a higher rate of return than impersonal solicitations. We expect that those who have given most often in the past, and at more levels of government, will be more likely to make a contribution in 1992. Further, we expect those with the highest incomes to be more likely to give again in 1992, in part because it is less of a sacrifice to do so. Finally, we expect those who lived in the home state of a candidate in 1988, and who therefore may have contributed because of some of the unique resources that home-state candidates can provide, would be less likely to respond in 1992.

To test these hypotheses, we used logistic regression to estimate the likelihood that an individual would contribute, if asked. The results are presented in Table 6.3. First, the coefficients for all the motivations are positive, although only the solidary motive is statistically significant. If we use *only* the motives to predict contributing, as shown in the top part of the table, the coefficient for each of the motives is positive and statistically significant, suggesting that many of the other variables in the model are intervening between motivations and the decision to give.

Although we do not find a significant relationship between purposive motives and giving, we do find as expected that extremism is correlated with giving. Extremism is an especially strong predictor of giving in response to impersonal solicitations. In the simple bivariate relationship, 52% of those who were extremely liberal or conservative gave in response to impersonal solicitations, compared to only 22% of moderates. From the overall logistic equation, we estimate that 74% of those who were extremely conservative or extremely liberal contributed, compared to 50% of moderates.[4]

Contributors who ranked high on our Index of Campaign Giving were more likely to give in 1992. Those who had never previously given more

Table 6.3. *Logistic regression predicting the decision to contribute if asked: Did the respondent give to any candidate in 1992?*

	b	se
Basic model		
Purposive	.15	.09[a]
Solidary	.35	.10[b]
Material	.17	.10[a]
Constant	.56	.09[b]
n	534	
Expanded model		
Purposive	.07	.11
Solidary	.21	.12[a]
Material	.11	.12
# 1992 impersonal solicitation	-.02	.07
# 1992 personal solicitations	.89	.17[b]
Index of campaign giving	.60	.14[b]
Index of campaign work	-.18	.15
Income	.11	.11
Missing on income dummy	.62	.53
Ideological extremism	.43	.14[b]
In home state in 1988	-.51	.25[a]
Constant	-3.93	.98[b]
n	504	

[a]Significant at .05 in a one-tail test.
[b]Significant at .01 in a one-tail test.
Logistic regression was used to estimate each equation.

than once to any level of office had a probability of contributing in 1992 of .40, compared to .76 for those who gave in most elections at all levels of office. In contrast, the Index of Campaign Work has no significant relationship with the likelihood of giving in 1992, once we have controlled for prior contribution patterns. The Index of Campaign Work is a significant predictor of giving in bivariate analysis, but once we hold constant contributing behavior this relationship disappears completely. Of course, working in politics and contributing are strongly related to each other, which means that those aspects of working that are not related to giving previously do not predict the decision to contribute.

In addition, the number of personal solicitations received is positively related to the decision to contribute, while the number of impersonal solicitations is unrelated. Individuals are more likely to toss letters in the trash than to hang up the phone on their friends and associates. Those who received no personal solicitations had a probability of contributing of only .53, compared to .71 for those who received one personal solicitation and .85 for those who received two. Wealthier members of the contributing pool showed little or no more likelihood than others to make a contribution in 1992. We explain this result in the next section.

Those who lived in the home state of the candidate to whom they contributed in 1988 were less likely to give in 1992. Using the logistic regression, we estimated their likelihood of giving was .55, compared to .65 for those who had not given to a home-state candidate. Quite simply, candidates in the home state of the contributor can offer benefits to the contributor that are not easily matched by out-of-state candidates. Thus these individuals are less likely to give in subsequent elections that typically involve solicitation by an out-of-state candidate.

Overall, then, the 1988 contributors who gave in response to a solicitation in 1992 were more likely to have a history of giving to campaigns. They were also more likely to have solidary motives and to have been solicited through personal networks – which underscores the efficiency of networking and the importance of the solidary motive in networking. They were also more likely to be ideologically extreme, because ideological extremism is a good indicator of a person's willingness to respond to a direct mail solicitation. Finally, as expected, they were less likely to have given to a home-state candidate in 1992.

How candidate characteristics influence who gives

Many contributors were solicited by more than one candidate and by different methods; therefore, they made several separate choices about whether to give to each candidate in response to a particular method of solicitation. Our second analysis seeks to model each decision made by members of the 1988 contributing pool in 1992. The unit of analysis is the solicitation by a candidate to a potential contributor. The primary reason for defining the unit of analysis as the candidate solicitation is to determine how the congruence between contributor perceptions of candidate ideology and the contributor's own ideological views influences the decision to give. Thus solicitations from different campaigns must be examined separately because the respondent may perceive different ideological distances to different candidates. Although our survey did not ask the number of solicitations that a contributor received from each candidate, we are able identify which campaigns successfully and unsuccessfully solicited each potential contributor, and by what methods they approached them. As we have shown, different candidate resources lead campaigns to use different solicitation methods that tap different mixes of motives in the contributing pool. We therefore estimate separate equations for impersonal solicitations and for personal solicitations. Overall, for each of these candidate solicitations, the probability of a contributor making a contribution to a campaign was .59 when that campaign approached the contributor using personal solicitations and was .25 when a campaign used impersonal methods.

In the data for these models, each potential contributor is represented by a separate record for each candidate who solicited him or her successfully, and by a separate record for each candidate who solicited unsuccessfully through the two major methods described in Chapter 4. These records will be identical on most variables, but because the candidate will differ, the values for ideological proximity will vary.

We expect that solidary and material motives will be positively related to a decision to make a contribution to a candidate in response to a personal solicitation, and that purposive motives will predict contributions in response to mail or telemarketing solicitations. Purposive motivations should lead to a contribution, however, only if the candidate is compatible with the contributor's ideology, since a contribution to a candidate with whom the contributor disagrees on policy does not further the purposive motivation. These data allow us to determine how the interaction between the purposive motivation and perceptions of candidate proximity on ideology affect the contribution decision. Solicitations from different candidates must be examined separately because the respondent may perceive different ideological distances to different candidates.

Most of the other variables in our predictive equation are the same as those for the equation in the preceding section. Our expectations regarding relationships are the same, with the following exceptions. In the previous case, we expected that the more solicitations an individual received, the more likely she or he was to give to at least one candidate. This expectation made sense, for the larger the set of candidates who approach a prospect, the more likely it is that at least one of them will be attractive enough to merit a contribution. In the present case, however, we expect that the sheer number of all candidate solicitations will be negatively related to a decision to contribute to any particular candidate. We suspect that some individuals who give to one candidate are less likely to give to the next candidate who asks. Some contributors may view the decision to give as a choice among candidates and make a commitment to only one candidate at a time.

In the previous analysis we expected that those with higher incomes would be more likely to contribute, but we found no relationship. However, in the present case we would expect an especially strong relationship between income and giving in response to personal solicitations because of the social and professional context within which networking occurs.

In addition to the variables used in the earlier model, this model contains measures of ideological distance, which we define as the absolute value of the difference between the respondent's self-placement on the seven-point liberalism–conservatism scale and the respondent's placement of the candidate who solicited her or him. For example, imagine a contributor who is solicited by two candidates; she perceives the first to be extremely liberal (1) and the other to be moderate (4). If this contributor considers herself to be slightly liberal (3), then she is one unit from the moderate candidate and two units from the extremely liberal candidate. Our measure is thus the number of units of distance between the contributor and the candidate. In addition, an interactive term was constructed by multiplying our measure of purposive motivation by ideological distance.

The results of the model predicting personal-network giving are reported in the first column of Table 6.4. Both solidary and material motives are positively related to the likelihood that a respondent contributes in response to a personal solicitation, though neither coefficient is statistically significant. If we use the motives alone to predict contributions, the coefficient is larger for material motives; however, it is still not statistically significant. Indeed, with the modest sample sizes in this portion of the analysis (we are looking only at instances of personal solicitation), quite large relationships are needed to achieve statistical significance.

The impact of the purposive motivation is best examined in conjunction with the ideological distance from the candidate who is soliciting a contribution, because there is a strong interaction between these two variables. Figure 6.1 shows the likelihood of making a contribution in response to a personal solicitation for individuals with various combinations of strength of purposive motivation and ideological proximity to the candidate who is soliciting them. Ideological distance matters greatly for those who have strong purposive motives. Individuals who are at the 75th percentile on purposive motivations give to 74% of the candidate requests when they perceive themselves to be at the same ideological position as the candidate requesting the contribu-

Table 6.4. *Logistic regression predicting for each campaign that solicited the respondent: Did the respondent give?*

	Solicited personally		Solicited impersonally	
	b	se	b	se
Purposive	.33	.22	.24	.17
Ideological distance	-.34	.14[b]	-.84	.13[b]
Purposive*ideological distance	-.28	.13[a]	-.31	.12[b]
Solidary	.18	.15	-.01	.11
Material	.09	.13	-.42	.12[b]
# 1992 solicitations	-.48	.13[b]	-.61	.13[b]
Index of campaign giving	-.04	.18	.48	.14[b]
Index of campaign work	-.08	.19	-.33	.14[b]
Income	.38	.14[b]	-.26	.10[b]
Ideological extremism	.04	.18	.64	.15[b]
In home state in 1988	-.16	.29	-1.03	.30[b]
Constant	.20	1.23	-2.51	1.05[b]
n	307		715	

[a]Significant at .05 in a one-tail test.
[b]Significant at .01 in a one-tail test.

tion. This likelihood of giving drops off rapidly with perceptions of increasing ideological distance. Those who perceive themselves to be two units away from a candidate on a seven-point scale give to 50% of requests, those four units away give to 26% of requests, and those six units away, the maximum distance, give to only 10% of requests. Among those contributors personally solicited *who care strongly about purposive motives*, there is a strong relationship between ideological proximity and contributing.

At first this may seem to contradict assertions about the importance of solidary and material motives made by the campaign finance specialists interviewed. However, among those people who care relatively little about purposive motives (those scoring at the 25th percentile on purposive motives), contributing is only weakly related to ideological distance. Among these individuals, those who perceive themselves to have the same ideological position as the candidate give 64% of the time, those two units away give 59% of the time, those four units away give 53% of the time, and

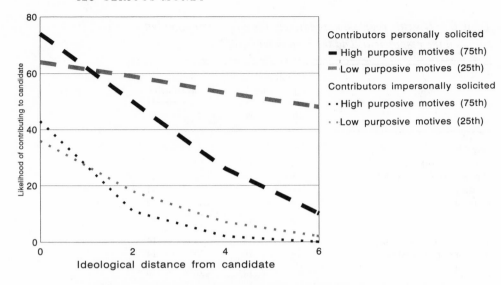

Figure 6.1. Predicting contributions: The influence of purposive motives and ideological distance. Numbers in legend refer to percentiles.

those six units away give 48% of the time. Thus we see only a slight drop-off in the likelihood of giving with increasing ideological distance among those who are influenced relatively little by purposive motives, compared to a very large drop off among those who are influenced a great deal by purposive motives.

In contrast, the bottom two lines of Figure 6.1 show that among those who are impersonally solicited, the likelihood of contributing drops off much more rapidly even among those who score relatively low on purposive motives. In general, perceived ideological distance matters more for those solicited impersonally than for those solicited personally. Although ideological distance matters less for those solicited personally and especially for those who care relatively less about purposive motives, it does matter to some extent even for these contributors. The bottom line is that ideological distance is important for all types of contributors, even though its importance varies greatly.

Although the data show that the likelihood of making a contribution diminishes with increasing ideological distance, this relationship is weaker among those who are personally solicited compared to those who are impersonally solicited. In the former case, it is in fact quite weak for those who score relatively low on purposive motives. Thus from the perspective of the networking campaign fundraiser, the likelihood of receiving a contribution from someone who is ideologically distant from your candidate is quite good among those who care little about purposive motives. Fully half of them will give to a candidate who is at the opposite end of the ideological spectrum. Even among those who care about ideology, and perceive the fundraiser's candidate to be two points distant, half will still make a contribution. These individuals are likely to perceive another candidate as ideologically more compatible, yet more of them will contribute in response to a personal solicitation from the first candidate than to an impersonal solicitation from a candidate with perfect ideological compatibility. It is thus easy to see why campaign fundraisers emphasize the importance of nonpurposive motives in successful personal solicitation. Candidate ideology does, however, matter, and sometimes quite a lot, in the likelihood of making a contribution in response to personal solicitations as well as impersonal ones.

As we expected, the more solicitations received, the less likely one is to respond to any particular solicitation. In addition, the likelihood of responding to a personal solicitation increases with income. It is among the wealthy that extensive personal relationships of reciprocal giving are developed. Also, since contributions made in response to a personal solicitation are typically larger than those given in response to an impersonal solicitation, the relationship with income is a sensible one. As we expected, contributors who lived in the home state of the candidate to whom they gave in 1988 were less likely than others to give in response to a personal solicitation in 1992. Many of the benefits associated with giving to a candidate in one's home state cannot be easily duplicated by out-of-state candidates.

The equation predicting contributions in response to impersonal solicitations is shown in the second column. Individuals who are motivated by solidary concerns are no more or less likely to give in response to impersonal solicitation, while those with material motives are much less likely to give in response to direct mail. The interaction between the purposive motivation and ideological proximity to the candidate is quite strong. Those at the 75th percentile on the purposive motivation give to 43% of the requests when they perceive themselves to be at the same ideological position as the candidate requesting the contribution. Those who perceive themselves to be two units away from a candidate on a seven-point scale give to 11% of requests, those four units away give to 2% of requests, and those six units away, the maximum distance, give to none of the requests. Thus we see an even sharper initial drop-off in giving with increasing ideological distance than we saw among those personally solicited.

Those individuals who are at the 25th percentile on the purposive motivation give to 36% of impersonal requests when they perceive themselves to be at the same ideological position as the candidate, contrasted to the 43% cited above among those at the 75th percentile. The drop-off in giving is less among those weakly motivated by purposive goals. Those who perceive themselves to be two units away from the candidate give to 18% of impersonal appeals; those four units to 7%; and those six units to 2%. Ideological distance matters less to those who are less strongly motivated by purposive motives. These results are quite sensible; purposive motives are the primary reward offered for giving impersonally, and those who are most strongly motivated are more likely to give when solicited by an ideologically compatible candidate than are those less strongly motivated.

As was the case for personal solicitations, it is also true for impersonal solicitations that the larger the number of candidates who approach a contributor, the less likely he or she is to respond to any specific candidate. Again we also find that those who lived in the home state of the candidate to whom they contributed in 1988 were less likely to give in response to a solicitation. In contrast to personal solicitations, we find that income has a negative relationship to giving in response to impersonal solicitations. Those with smaller incomes are actually more likely to respond to an impersonal solicitation than are the wealthy, who are more likely to receive and to respond to personal solicitations. It must be remembered, of course, that this sample consists of relatively wealthy individuals who give to presidential campaigns. Thus among this affluent population, those with less impressive incomes are more responsive than their wealthier counterparts to the emotional appeals of direct mail solicitation.

We find that those who rank high on the Index of Campaign Giving are again more likely to contribute in response to an impersonal solicitation than those who rank low on this measure. We also find that individuals who give in most elections to all types of office give to 33% of candidates who make an impersonal request. Those who have given no more than once to candidates seeking any office give to only 15% of candidates who ask them impersonally. Controlling for the extent of giving, the Index of Campaign Work is actually negatively related to impersonal giving. The aspect of political participation that is relevant to donating in response to impersonal solicitation is the pattern of prior contributions, not campaign participation in general. In contrast, neither giving nor working has any significant relationship with giving in response to personal solicitations.

Finally, we also see that ideological extremism is positively related to giving in response to impersonal solicitations. There is no relationship between extremism and giving in response to personal solicitations. Those who are most ideologically extreme give to 38% of impersonal requests; moderates give to 12%. This result also fits our expectations. Campaign finance officials interviewed indicated that more ideologically extreme candidates have greater success than moderate candidates in making impersonal fundraising appeals.

In sum, these data show that ideological distance is important in making decisions about whether to give to a particular candidate. It is especially important for those who are motivated by purposive concerns and who are solicited impersonally. But even among those who are solicited personally and are not especially motivated by purposive considerations, ideological distance is still a significant predictor of the decision to give.

The solicitors – Who is asked to solicit contributions?

In Chapter 4 we described in detail the structure of personal networks. The success of such networks depends critically on the willingness of some individuals to ask others to give. Top solicitors must spend of much of their time locating other solicitors. Although pyramids differ in their depth, all depend on the willingness of some contributors to ask others to solicit as well as to give.

We asked respondents in 1992 whether they were asked to solicit on behalf of a candidate, and in both 1988 and 1992 we asked whether they did solicit. The campaign finance officials interviewed agreed that no one solicits without being asked, and the data confirm this, showing that only 1% of the solicitors indicated that they had solicited without being asked.[5] Thus our first step in studying the decision to solicit is to examine, as we did with contributors, who is targeted to solicit.

Campaigns seek solicitors who have the social skills to raise money. These skills are more likely to be found among those who enjoy social contacts, and we therefore expect them to ask people with solidary motives to solicit. Campaigns also seek people who can build on networks of reciprocity, and such individuals are more likely to be found among those who have material motives. Our interviews with campaign professionals would suggest little relationship with purposive motivations. Our findings regarding the importance of purposive motivations in explaining contributing behavior in social networks suggest, however, that we should find a positive relationship.

Table 6.5 shows the results of two logistic regression equations predicting who was asked to solicit in 1992. The first equation included only our measures of the motives as independent variables. The results in this first equation show that the more strongly a contributor is motivated by solidary and materi-

Table 6.5. *Logistic regression predicting whether respondent was asked to solicit others*

	b	se
Basic model		
Purposive	.10	.10
Solidary	.29	.10^b
Material	.27	.10^b
Constant	-1.13	.10^b
Expanded model		
Purposive	.14	.11
Solidary	.20	.13
Material	.12	.11
Index of campaign giving	.18	.15
Index of campaign work	.15	.13
Income < $50,000	-1.43	.57^b
Income $50,000 – $99,999	-0.02	.42
Income $100,000 – $249,999	.02	.38
Income $250,000 and over	.38	.38
Did R solicit in 1988	.69	.24^b
Constant	-2.13	.53^b
n	500	

^{a}Significant at .05 in a one-tail test.
^{b}Significant at .01 in a one-tail test.

al concerns, the more likely it is that he or she will be asked to solicit others. The purposive motivation shows a weaker and not statistically significant relationship, although it is positive. These findings fit with our expectations.

We can gain more insight into the targeting decisions of campaigns by examining some of the specific means by which potential solicitors with particular motives can be identified. Campaign finance figures interviewed said that top solicitors tend to recruit those who have solicited before, and our data show that there is some continuity between those who solicited in 1988 and those who were asked to do so in 1992. Thirty-nine percent of those who solicited in 1988 were again asked to solicit in 1992, while only 19% of those contributors who had not solicited in 1988 were approached in 1992. Thus those who solicited in 1988 were twice as likely to be asked to do so in 1992 as nonsolicitors.

These numbers are probably depressed by the nature of the Republican competition in 1992. Buchanan, as an ideological candidate, did not attempt to build personal networks. Bush, who networked extensively in 1988, first attempted to mobilize his 1988 personal network by mail. As Philip Smith noted, all of those who attended a Bush event in 1988 were mailed to in 1992, and our data show that more than a third of those who contributed through Bush's personal network in 1988 were successfully solicited by mail in 1992. The funds raised through these mailings reduced his need to rely on personal networking to the extent he did in 1988. Thus many of the potential solicitors in the Republican party were not asked to solicit in 1992 – and, moreover, it must be kept in mind that 1992 had far fewer candidates than 1988. The data bear out this hypothesis: 50% of the Democrats who had solicited before were asked to solicit again, compared with 27% of the Republicans.

Our interviews with campaign finance officials indicate that all solicitors are themselves contributors first. Thus the solicitors are a subset of the larger pool of contributors. Solicitors, however, are not asked to solicit the following election year to the same extent contributors are asked to contribute. Although nearly 90% of the contributing pool from 1988 were asked to give again in 1992, only half of the Democratic pool of solicitors were asked to solicit again. The most likely explanation for this discrepancy is the greater fragility of personal networks. All contributors, regardless of the means of initial contact, eventually appear on a candidate list and can therefore easily be solicited again through the mail. However, it usually requires a personal contact by someone with a special relationship to induce someone to solicit. If someone near the top of a personal network decides to sit out an election, it is very difficult to find anyone who can fully activate that solicitor's portion of the network, and to approach all of those whom she had asked to solicit in past elections. Solicitors near the top of personal networks invest large amounts of time, energy, and social capital, and many endure a significant reduction in personal income by taking time from work. The burnout and dropout rate among these top solicitors is therefore relatively high. As a result, much larger gaps inevitably appear in the pyramid of solicitors than in the lists of contributors.

This means that there is a constant need to recruit new solicitors. Fully half of those asked to solicit in 1992 had not solicited in 1988. Since all solicitors are contributors first, it is logical for campaigns to recruit new solicitors from the pool of regular contributors; it also makes sense to recruit solicitors from among those who work in politics. We therefore hypothesize that the more individuals work and give in politics, the more likely they are to be asked to solicit on behalf of a candidate.

Finally, we would expect that wealthier contributors would be more likely to be asked to solicit than would contributors of more modest means. It is logical for campaigns to ask wealthy contributors to solicit because those who can afford to give money are best able to ask others for money. Wealthy contributors are more likely to have the types of relationships with others that are the basis for soliciting contributions, and they are more likely to know people who, like themselves, can afford to give.

The lower half of Table 6.5 shows the results of this second logistic regression equation predicting whether or not a contributor was asked to solicit. The coefficients for the motives are all positive but no longer statistically significant. Those who solicited in 1988 were significantly more likely to do so again in 1992. Solicitors are recruited from those who have frequently given to and worked for campaigns and parties in the past. Our measures of these variables are moderately correlated with each other, and although they are not significant individually, they are significant taken together.[6] Income has been included as a set of dichotomous dummy variables, with the residual category being those who did not disclose their income, therefore allowing us to include this group in the analysis.[7] Income shows a strong monotonic relationship with being asked to solicit. The larger one's income, the more likely one is to be asked to solicit others. These results are thus consistent with our basic theoretical expectations: solicitors are recruited from those who have solicited before, those who contribute and work most frequently in campaigns, and those who are wealthy.

The solicitors – Who agrees to solicit contributions?

Who decides to solicit? Overall, 40% of those asked do in fact agree ($n = 130$). This success rate indicates that the targeting analyzed in the previous section must be quite efficient. This is especially impressive, given the constant need to recruit many new solicitors.

Large numbers of solicitors are needed because most solicitors approach only a few prospects. Although a few of our contributors report having asked many others to give, the median solicitor in our sample reported asking only twelve people to contribute, six of whom actually gave. Our sample reflects the nature of a personal network pyramid. A few contributors, especially those at the top, have large numbers of contacts they can solicit for the candidate. But most solicitors are found at the bottom of the pyramid, and these individuals approach only a small number of other people.

Table 6.6. *Logistic regression predicting among those asked to solicit: Who solicited?*

	b	se
Basic model		
Purposive	.20	.20
Solidary	.37	.20[a]
Material	.45	.19[b]
Constant	-.64	.20[b]
Expanded model		
Purposive	.17	.23
Solidary	.28	.24
Material	.42	.22[a]
Index of campaign giving	.51	.31[a]
Index of campaign work	.21	.27
Income < $50,000	-.52	1.73
Income $50,000 – $99,999	1.59	.91[a]
Income $100,000 – $249,999	1.20	.80
Income $250,000 and over	2.22	.83[b]
Did R solicit in 1988	.56	.50
Constant	-4.44	1.23[b]
n	128	

[a]Significant at .05 in a one-tail test.
[b]Significant at .01 in a one-tail test.

Once a contributor has been asked to solicit on behalf of a candidate, he or she must decide whether or not to do so. Based on our earlier discussion of personal networks in Chapter 4, we would expect the material and to a lesser extent solidary motives to be strongly associated with the decision to solicit. In the preceding sections of this chapter, we found that purposive motives were also related to decisions to give in personal networks, and so we expect that they may be weakly related to the decision to solicit as well.[8]

Table 6.6 shows at the top a logistic regression predicting the likelihood of soliciting for a candidate if asked, using the three motives as independent variables. These data should be taken as suggestive because of the small sample of individuals who were asked to solicit. Even with our small sample size, we find both material and solidary motives to be strongly and significantly associated with a willingness to solicit.

It is understandable that those who agree to solicit have solidary motives. As we have argued above, those who are willing to ask others for money almost certainly are to be found among those who enjoy social contacts, and, as discussed in Chapter 4, campaigns also build pyramids of personal solicitors around a range of rewards tied to forms of special recognition. Successfully raising money is an excellent way of earning recognition.

It is also understandable that those with material motives will be willing to solicit. For example, given the $1,000 limit on contributions, the only way to make a memorable donation to the campaign kitty is to solicit successfully a large number of other people to contribute – either directly or by recruiting yet others to solicit beneath one in the pyramid. To the extent that those with material motives desire access to a policy maker, and to the extent that the degree of access is related to the amount of money a person raises on behalf of that policy maker's campaign, becoming a solicitor is one of the few ways to be a major player in the access game.

The coefficient for the purposive motive is positive but much weaker and not statistically significant. It is possible that we might have discovered an interaction effect between purposive motives and ideological distance from the candidate similar to that above, but we could not test for this with these data.

The lower half of Table 6.6 shows the full multivariate analysis. Despite the difficulties of activating former solicitors, we expect that they will be more likely than others to solicit again. Also, we expect in general that those who give the most extensively and work the most extensively in politics will be more likely to solicit than those who don't. Finally, those who are wealthy themselves will be more likely to have personal contacts who can be easily solicited and will thus be more willing to do so.

Because only 130 respondents were asked to solicit, the number of cases in this analysis is small. The small sample size prevents relatively robust relationships from achieving statistical significance. The material motive remains a strong and significant predictor of soliciting. The solidary motive also shows a reasonably large positive coefficient, and the purposive motive a much smaller one, although neither of these coefficients is statistically significant. The coefficient for those who have solicited in the past is in the correct direction and is reasonably large in magnitude, but it, too, is not statistically significant. The Index of Campaign Giving and the Index of Campaign Work are positively related to soliciting, although only the large coefficient for giving is significant.

It is interesting that the coefficients for past giving and working in campaigns were of roughly similar magnitude in predicting who is asked to solicit, but the decision to solicit is much more strongly related to previous patterns of giving than to previous patterns of working. This reinforces our interpretation of soliciting as an activity more strongly related to giving money in politics than to working in politics. Finally, we find that the larger the income of the contributor, the more likely he or she is to agree to solicit others.

Thus we find that the variables that are related to targeting potential solicitors are strongly related to whether or not an individual agrees to solicit, which tends to confirm the hypothesis that those who ask others to solicit are well-informed about the people they are recruiting. The relationships are actually weaker in this model than they would have been had we predicted soliciting from the entire sample, regardless of whether the individual was asked. And of course, including in the model a measure of whether the respondent had solicited in 1988 would diminish the impact of many of the other independent variables that were important factors in influencing the decision to solicit in 1992. We also predicted who among all respondents had solicited in 1988, and we did find generally stronger relationships than those shown in Table 6.6.

Conclusions

Although candidates often hope to attract new contributors and solicitors, they rely primarily on the continuing pool of contributors to finance their campaigns and to populate their networks. They must develop a strategy to identify and solicit contributors, and to identify and approach those who will ask others for money. Individuals must in turn decide whether they will give to each candidate who asks, and whether they are willing to spend the time and social capital to solicit for that candidate if they are asked to do so.

Our data suggest that almost all members of the contributing pool are solicited by at least one candidate, and that many are asked to give to more than one campaign. Candidates mail to lists of past contributors, but it appears that those who are contacted through personal networks and those who have the strongest history of giving at all levels of politics are the most likely to give. Although those who are solicited through personal networks do give across parties and across the ideological spectrum, our data indicate that for many of these individuals, ideological compatibility with the candidate is a necessary precondition for giving. This is especially true for those who are motivated by purposive considerations, and even more for those who are solicited through the mail or telemarketing.

The contributing pool also provides the recruiting ground for potential solicitors. Those who are most active in politics, especially those who have solicited before, are likely to be asked to solicit again, as are wealthy individuals who can tap wealthy friends and business associates. Among those asked to solicit, those who are wealthier, motivated by material concerns, and have been especially active in contributing or soliciting in the past are more likely to agree to ask others to contribute.

7. Conclusion

The campaign finance process unfolds as an interaction of two sets of decisions, one by the campaigns, and the other by potential contributors. Campaigns must assess their resources and identify their most likely financial constituencies. They must then determine the best methods to approach these constituencies, considering carefully the likely motives of those whom they hope will contribute to their candidates, and the benefits that their resources allow them to offer to those potential contributors. Potential contributors must decide whether to contribute to a candidate and how much to give. More than a third of contributors are asked to give to more than one candidate, and these contributors must make separate but possibly related decisions about giving to each candidate who asked them.

Campaigns that build personal-solicitation networks must also decide which of their contributors they will ask to solicit on behalf of others. Campaigns with relatively broad pyramids rely on fewer solicitors, but ask that they each raise proportionately more money. Campaigns with relatively deep pyramids rely on more solicitors, who must therefore raise proportionately less money. Those who are asked to solicit must decide whether to spend the social, political, and occasionally economic capital to become more involved in the campaign. They presumably assess the likely benefits of active participation, and may consider the probability that the candidate will win.

The decisions by campaigns are constrained by two sets of factors: the legal regulatory structure, and the need to solicit largely from the existing pool of contributors. The rules limit the maximum size of the contribution, therefore creating the need to solicit at a minimum tens of thousands of potential donors. They also provide matching funds for small gifts, making it possible for candidates with strong appeal to the ideological wings of their party to finance their campaigns through many small contributions that are effectively doubled by the federal government.

Our data show that all campaigns in 1988 raised serious money primarily in contributions from an existing pool of contributors, many of whom have given in some but not all elections. Candidates do seek to expand the pool by attracting contributions from among individuals who have never before given to presidential candidates, primarily by soliciting those who have regularly given to other political and social causes. Yet even Robertson and Jackson, who attempted to mobilize clearly identifiable constituencies in the voting booths, relied primarily on contributions from members of the pool when it came to raising serious money. Almost all members of the pool are asked to give in subsequent elections, and those who give most regularly to all kinds of candidates and party committees are likely to receive solicitations from several candidates.

This pool of regular contributors is composed of individuals with different mixes of motives: some seek primarily economic advantage for their firms or themselves, others value the opportunity to interact with those who share their partisanship and social characteristics, and still others seek to achieve various policy goals, primarily by electing candidates who share their views. These material, solidary, and purposive motives shape their contribution behavior, and their responses to appeals from different types of candidates.

Faced with these two constraints, campaigns have developed two primary ways of soliciting contributions. Some rely on large contributions raised through networks of personal solicitors; others fund their campaigns through smaller gifts raised through direct mail or telemarketing. Campaigns generally do a little of both, but nearly all of the campaigns in our study focused most of their time and capital on one method of solicitation. Because campaigns seek to raise the maximum amounts for the smallest expenditure of resources, the decision generally reflects what works best for the candidate.

Different methods work better for different candidates because of the resources these candidates possess. Candidates who can dispense material or solidary benefits rely primarily on personal-solicitation networks, which raise substantial sums quickly and at relatively low cost. Because the maximum allowable contribution has not been adjusted for inflation in two decades, campaigns have over time increasingly relied on these personal networks. Thus sitting governors, members of Congress, and those with access to party networks now generally choose to rely primarily on personal-solicitation networks.

In contrast, those candidates whose appeal is to the ideological wing of their parties rely on direct mail and telemarketing to attract small contributions from many individuals. Although the value of matching funds has also eroded with inflation, in 1988 these impersonal methods of solicitation remained viable ways to finance campaigns. Indeed, Robertson raised more money than any other candidate in the race, and Jackson raised enough money to allow him to finish second to Dukakis for the Democratic nomination.

Although we have described the choice of the method of solicitation as a decision made by the campaign, in most instances it is a preordained one. Bush and Dukakis could not have financed their campaigns through direct mail, and Robertson and Jackson could not have successfully built large national networks. It is the resources of the candidates that determine the types of financial constituencies they can build, and the methods they must use to build them.

We have identified several resources that candidates relied upon in 1988. Most relied on in-state supporters to fund the early parts of their campaign. Candidates mail to the lists of home-state contributors who have supported their earlier campaigns, and these "house lists" are generally quite profitable. They also build in-state networks, generally based on material or solidary benefits that sitting governors and members of congress can provide. Home-state money is especially vital to lesser-known candidates, who use this seed money to gain name recognition.

In addition, there are several resources that are best exploited through national networks. These include close relationships with party activists and officials, congressional office, and racial, ethnic, and religious identities. Candidates with these resources generally rely on personal solicitation to mobilize support, dispensing solidary and purposive benefits to party activists and material benefits to lobbyists and corporate executives. They tap racial, ethnic, and religious identities through a mix of solidary, material, and purposive benefits.

Finally, the policy positions of candidates are resources in attracting money from the contributing pool. Candidates spend much time and money subtly positioning themselves to attract funds from contributors, and we argue that ideology is a resource for moderate and extreme candidates alike. Contributors are a well-informed, sophisticated, and select group, and they are able to distinguish among candidate positions on a number of issues. Contributors who value purposive benefits generally support candidates who share many of their views. There are therefore clear differences in candidate ideological constituencies which mirror the differences in positions that the candidates staked during the campaign. Our data suggest that campaign finance professionals may underestimate the role of ideology in personal networks, for those solicited in person by someone they know are more likely to give if that candidate shares their partisan and ideological positions.

This latter point is worth emphasizing. Although some of the campaign finance professionals we interviewed seemed to suggest that campaign receipts were purely a function of their solicitation skills, in fact the issue positions that candidates take affect who contributes to their campaigns. Very few contributors give to candidates with whom they are in fundamental ideological disagreement.

Our findings have a number of implications for governance, for politics, and for future research. In the remainder of this chapter, we explore those implications.

Implications for governance

The two major methods of solicitation identified in Chapter 4 each raise different normative problems. Although our data show that purposive motives are important in personal networks, they also confirm the view of those we interviewed that such networks are based disproportionately on material benefits and to a lesser extent solidary benefits. Campaign finance professionals who specialized in networks and others who specialized in mail told us that the bottom of personal-solicitation pyramids is composed of those who cannot say no to those who ask them. One direct mail specialist told us that if he were asked to raise $25,000 for a candidate, he would contact the twenty-five printers who printed his letters and envelopes, for they would find it difficult to refuse a request. Michael Berman, a personal-network specialist who raised money for Humphrey and Mondale, noted that people give for three reasons – for love, for money, and for me. By the generic "me," Berman meant that the contributor could not refuse a request by the solicitor. One direct mail specialist characterized these networks as based on fear – fear that the potential contributor might lose the business of the solicitor, that she or he might be passed over for promotion by the executive who asked for her or his gift, or that she or he might lose social status by failing to appear at a fundraising dinner. We do not wish to overstate this, but it is one of the realities of personal-network fundraising.

Moreover, at the top of these networks are professional fundraisers, many of whom are lawyer-lobbyists who hope to represent their clients to the candidate for whom they are soliciting. Thus many of those who gave to Gephardt and especially Dole were not fully interested in whether the candidate won the presidency, for access to those who controlled the congressional agenda was potentially at least as valuable. This access may come at a public price. When we say that sitting governors or members of Congress dispense material benefits, we are saying that at least some contributors have received particularistic benefits from the public purse.

Finally, those who are able to contribute $1,000 to a presidential candidate through personal networks are mostly affluent, white male professionals or business executives. Although scholars have been very interested in the problem of democratic representation in primary and caucus electorates, it should be noted that the gaps between all citizens and general-election voters, and between general-election voters and primary-election voters, are much smaller than between any of these groups and campaign contributors. Because voters tend to be of higher socioeconomic status than nonvoters, it can be argued that the system tends to neglect the interests of the poor. To the extent that contributors are influential actors, their substantial socioeconomic advantages should raise even greater concern among democratic theorists. Counterbalancing this concern, at least in the Democratic party, is the fact that contributors of serious money appear to be much more sympathetic to the interests of minorities than are Democratic primary and general-election voters.

At first glance, it might seem that money raised through direct mail is preferable to funds raised through personal networks. Citizens who give through the mail are less affluent and are generally seeking some kind of public good rather than a personal financial reward. Yet as one direct mail specialist (who asked not to be identified) noted, "issue-oriented money" can also create problems for the political system. First, candidates who raise their money by direct mail may actually be led to take more extreme positions to increase their fundraising prospects, which makes them less electable in November and perhaps less able to govern if they win. In addition, direct mail money is principally available only to ideologically extreme candidates and therefore pushes the political system away from the center. Third, the ideologically extreme contributors who give in response to direct mail appeals are unlikely to support the compromises that are an integral part of the American political system, therefore limiting the flexibility and likely effectiveness of their candidate.

It should be noted that these two fundraising techniques are not unique to presidential campaigns but are used by candidates for other offices, and by political causes in general. Thus the same troubling normative issues are relevant to political campaigns at all levels of government. It is these normative issues that are typically cited by proponents of publicly financed campaigns, although public financing has its own problems, including the cost to the treasury and strong public opposition.

There are few viable alternatives to networking and mass mail appeals. They are basic not only to political fundraising but to virtually all kinds of public fundraising. Indeed, Patrick Shields, who has raised money for various educational and medical nonprofit organizations, told us that social and philanthropic fundraising depends almost entirely on the two fundraising techniques discussed in Chapter 4.

Implications for politics

Our study has political implications as well. First, as primary elections and caucuses become increasingly front-loaded, the value of an early fundraising start is enhanced. Those candidates who can raise substantial sums early from within their home states have a clear advantage over those who are unable to do so. Sitting governors and to a lesser extent senators have the ability to provide solidary and especially material benefits to home-state contributors, and have ready mailing lists of supporters who will give to their campaigns. Moreover, candidates who can mobilize money from wealthy states have an advantage over those who come from less affluent states. Sitting governors from large states therefore can extract far more wealth from their states than other candidates, and thus can gather the necessary seed money to launch their campaigns. As we noted in Chapter 5, Dukakis and Gephardt raised a similar amount before July 1, 1987, from outside their state, yet Dukakis had a nearly $2 million advantage in home-state funds. This advantage alone was nearly twice the total receipts of the Gephardt campaign from both inside and outside Missouri.

Of course, an in-state base is not essential to raising early money. In 1988, Robertson also was able to raise substantial early cash, but in this case the money came from people across the country who had signed his petition to run for office and who had typically given regularly to his television program. Dole mobilized his national network early as well, building on his resources as a powerful Senate leader. Nonetheless, the front-loaded calendar advantages candidates who can raise money early, and candidates with a large home-state base find it easiest to do so.

Second, as the value of the $1,000 maximum contribution erodes from inflation, but the overall spending cap grows with inflation, campaigns need to reach more contributors or convince contributors to give larger amounts – ideally the maximum amount. Our data suggest that there is a clear trend toward increasing reliance on personal networks to meet increasing cash demands. Indeed, the 1992 Bush campaign appeared to accept matching funds almost as an afterthought, and concentrated instead on raising as many $1,000 contributions as possible. Unless the contribution limit or matching fund limit is raised, it seems likely that this trend will continue.

Pyramids therefore will need to reach ever larger numbers of contributors. This will increase the value of those solicitors who can build larger and more effective pyramids. These financial intermediaries have already replaced the "fat cats" of the past in importance, and appear likely to become even more vital to the conduct of modern campaigns in the future.

Although pyramids appear to be increasingly popular fundraising tools, direct mail and telemarketing are still used extensively, most often in recent years by ideologically extreme candidates. Federal matching funds help make profitable the development of mailing lists that over time influence the character of the contributing pool. Once an individual has given to a presidential candidate, his or her name will appear on a list that will be rented to others. These individuals will be solicited again by presidential candidates, and most likely by candidates for other offices as well. Many will decide to give to other candidates. Thus the federal match indirectly subsidizes the creation of widely available lists of ideologically motivated contributors who will give to candidates and organizations who share their views.

Implications for future research

Although our data have provided a much clearer picture of the motivations and decisions of contributors, and to a lesser extent of campaigns, our study has also raised many questions. Our surveys were by necessity exploratory, for there was little theory or research to guide us. There is still much to be learned about individual contributors. Our data provide the basis of comparison for future studies of different sets of contributors and other kinds of campaign activists. We think that four kinds of comparative studies might expand our understanding of campaign finance.

First, and perhaps most important, our results for those who give serious money should be compared to those who make smaller gifts. Although our data suggest that those who made smaller donations to Robertson, Kemp, and Jackson did not differ significantly from those who gave larger sums, our sample included only those whose gifts eventually aggregated to at least $201 to at least one candidate. It is likely that those who make a single small gift to a presidential nomination candidate differ in their demographic characteristics, their motivations, their level and types of political participation, and in their political views from those who give serious money. We sampled contributors whose names appeared on published lists at the FEC, but since we conducted our survey, the commission has made available lists of contributors of small amounts, whose contributions were matched by the federal government. It is also possible to rent lists used by campaigns, thereby reaching these donors of smaller sums.

In addition to studying those who make small contributions, it would be interesting to compare the contributing pool to the smaller subset who give soft money or who give to candidate PACs and foundations. Nearly all of these individuals appear on the lists from which we drew our sample, for in all likelihood they made hard money contributions to campaign committees as well. But there are relatively few of these kinds of contributors overall, and there are therefore few of them in our sample. Thus we are not able to profile them and examine whether and how they may differ from the rest of the contributing pool. Green and Guth (1988a, 1988b) have surveyed contributors to presidential PACs, but to date there has been no scholarly investigation of contributors of soft money or of those who give to the foundations associated with presidential candidates. The FEC has lists of contributors of soft money and of those who give to presidential PACs, but there are no readily available lists of those who give to candidate foundations. Such lists may be available for rent.

In addition to comparing contributors of serious money to other kinds of presidential givers, they should be compared with those who give to congressional candidates, party committees, and PACs. Although we are able to identify who among the presidential contributors gives to these other committees, our sample does not include those who gave to congressional candidates, parties, or PACs – but not to presidential candidates. A good deal of work has been done on contributors to these other campaign finance actors (Biersack, Herrnson, Joe, and Wilcox 1994; Green and Guth 1986, 1988a, 1988b; Powell 1989) but it is now time to begin to make comparisons of the results of surveys of these various kinds of contributors, as Jones and Miller (1985) have done using NES data.

Third, it would be interesting to determine the extent to which the culture of giving is broadly generalized. Our data show that a majority of members of the presidential pool give at least occasionally to other kinds of candidates and political causes, and the anecdotal evidence suggests that there is a norm of reciprocity in personal solicitation networks that involves political, cultural, and philanthropic giving. It may be that some individuals have a general propensity to contribute to causes they believe in, while others are more narrowly focused on political concerns. Comparing contributors to political campaigns to those who give to other social causes might prove instructive.

Finally, because solicitors play an increasingly important role in presidential campaign finance, a survey of these financial intermediaries would potentially be quite valuable. Our interviews suggested that solicitors' motives vary with their location in the pyramid, and a more focused study of these individuals could confirm or disprove this claim. Moreover, it would be interesting to examine the contacts between solicitors and candidates (especially winning candidates) after the election.

In addition to future research comparing serious money contributors to those who participate in campaigns in different ways, it would be helpful to study contribution behavior throughout the course of a campaign. The presidential nomination process is a dynamic one, and contributors make many decisions over the two years during which it unfolds. During this time, many things can change: the composition of the candidate field, the candidates' electoral prospects, the salience of national and local issues, and the issue positions candidates use to define themselves and other candidates. Contributors may be solicited at different times during the election cycle, perhaps by different candidates, and so the decisions and evaluations that underlie those decisions will change as well. A panel study with data collected at several times during the election cycle would permit us to understand better the dynamics of contributor decisions.

The value of such a study would be enhanced by interviews with the chief fundraisers of campaigns at the same time the survey data are collected. This would enable us to understand the subtle interplay between the decisions of the campaigns and those of the contributors. Since media coverage influences potential campaign contributors, an analysis of the content of media coverage at these time points would also be valuable in understanding the decisions of contributors.

Finally, our interview data suggest that personal networks frequently work within single companies, industries, and corporate supply networks. This confirms journalistic accounts that interest groups play a far larger role in presidential finance than simple reports of PAC contributions would indicate. Our data can only hint at coordinated interest-group giving, but a different sampling frame would permit a fuller investigation of this phenomenon.

Appendix I
The 1988 and 1992 presidential nomination surveys

The 1988 survey was conducted by the authors. We drew a random sample of contributions to each of the eleven major presidential nomination candidates in the 1988 election. These candidates were: Babbitt, Bush, Dole, du Pont, Dukakis, Gephardt, Gore, Jackson, Kemp, Robertson, and Simon. The sample was drawn from the lists of contributors that candidates filed with the Federal Election Commission (FEC), and was based on pre-July 1988 contributions that aggregated to over $200 to a single candidate.

We received completed surveys from 1,246 respondents, representing a response rate of 37%. Our estimate of response rate was a conservative one. We did eliminate known invalid addresses (of contributors who had moved without forwarding addresses, or whose forwarding addresses had expired, or whose addresses were incorrectly recorded by the campaign committees to begin with), together with deceased or hospitalized contributors. However, we are confident that the 37% is a lower bound for the response rate because we certainly have not identified all of the inappropriate addresses or deceased or ill respondents.

Although this is not a high response rate, it is not unusual for this type of survey or sample. Two preceding surveys of contributors, one of 1972 presidential contributors and another of 1978 House contributors, produced response rates of approximately 50%. (See Brown, Hedges, and Powell, 1980a, for the 1972 survey and Powell, 1989, for the 1978 survey.) However, responses to all types of surveys (mail, telephone, and in-person) have dropped sharply in recent years, and our results reflect that. Guth and Greene (1991), surveying a similar population, were able to get a 40% response rate with five mailings and an elimination of institutional addresses. They found few differences between respondents to a fourth and fifth mailing compared to earlier mailings, suggesting that a greater effort to increase the response rate marginally has little additional benefit in enhancing the representativeness of the sample.

Two weight variables were used in our analysis: (1) From the lists we obtained a sample of contributions. However, unweighted data based on a sample of contributions would give an individual who appeared twice on the list double the likelihood of being sampled compared to an individual who appeared only once. We wished to weight our data to compensate for this. That is, if 10% of contributors gave once, they should, after weighting, appear to constitute 10% of our data set. If the data were not weighted, individuals who gave many contributions would "count" for much more than they should, and individuals who gave only once would "count" for less than they should. Using survey items that asked the contributors how many times they gave and how much they gave, together with the FEC reports themselves, we estimated the number of times each contributor appeared on a candidate's list. We used these estimates to weight the data to compensate for the increased likelihood of sampling a multiple contributor from the candidate list. Individuals were therefore weighted in inverse proportion to the number of times we estimated them to appear on a candidate's lists. This weight was used in any analysis where breakdowns were made by candidate. (2) In addition, a second weight was constructed when we wished to profile all the contributors taken as a whole or in analyses where all contributors to all candidates were combined. This weight had two components. One component was similar to that described above. Contributors were weighted in inverse proportion to the number of times they appeared on *all* candidates' lists. The second component was designed to weight each candidate's contributors in proportion to the percent of all contributors giving to that candidate. Because we oversampled those candidates who had few contributors in order to have enough respondents to analyze the results on a candidate-by-candidate basis, analyses of total overall contributors needed to be based on a weighted sample that reflected our estimate of the total distribution of contributors among the eleven candidates sampled. This estimate of the distribution of contributors of more than $200 between the candidates was calculated on the basis of a formula that uses the FEC final report of the distribution (by candidate) of contributions of $500 or more, and the ratio of the number of contributors of $500 or more to each candidate to the total number of contributors of over $200 to each candidate obtained from the original sample drawn for each candidate from the FEC lists.

We estimate that contributors of more than $200 to these eleven candidates represent more than 90% of the total of contributors of more than $200

to all major party-candidates. The only major-party candidates whose contributors were not surveyed were Joe Biden (who had quit the race before the
first event), Hart (who had quit the previous summer and then reentered, but
who, in his second try, raised less than $150,000), Lyndon La Rouche, and
Alexander Haig (who raised the smallest amount of any major-party candidate). We believe that our sample can be taken as generally representative of
all contributors of more than $200 to major-party candidates.

We resurveyed our 1988 respondents after the 1992 election, asking them
questions about which of the 1992 candidates had solicited them, how they
were solicited, and to which solicitations they had responded. In addition we
asked them if they had been asked to solicit others and if they had done so.
We received 583 completed surveys. Our response rate had a lower bound of
53%. This is a very conservative lower bound because some of our earlier
respondents had moved and either left no forwarding address or missed the
time limit for forwarding information. Others had died or were too ill to
complete a survey. Those whom we could not contact were counted in the
computation of the response rate and thus lowered it substantially.

The 1988 and 1992 survey items that were analyzed in this book are
shown in Appendix II.

Appendix II

1988 and 1992 survey items used in analysis

1988 SURVEY ITEMS USED IN ANALYSIS

Issue and ideological items

The issue and ideological items were asked in three different formats, as follows:

Agree–disagree items:

For the first set of items, respondents were given the following five choices: agree strongly; agree somewhat; neither agree nor disagree; disagree somewhat; disagree strongly. These items included

• Reducing the budget deficit should be the next president's top priority.
• The next president should raise taxes to help balance the budget.
• Free trade is important, even if it results in the loss of U.S. jobs.
• This country would be better off if it returned to the gold standard.
• The government should provide a program of health insurance for those not currently insured.
• Mandatory death penalty for murder should be the law.
• Defense spending should be reduced.
• We should have mandatory prayer in the public schools.
• The government should not regulate what adults read, even if that includes pornography.
• Child care is the parents' responsibility; government should not be involved.
• Students or teachers should not be required to pledge allegiance to the flag.
• Businesses should have the right to test any employee for drug use whenever they choose.
• The government should prohibit abortion.

Seven- point issue and ideological scales
The second set of items used a seven- point scale. Many of those items were replicated from the National Election Study (NES) items. On the liberalism–conservatism scales each of the seven scale points was labeled as shown below. On the other items, only the end points were labeled, as is the practice in the NES for these items. The text of the first item is shown in detail, and the exact format of the item is shown for the respondent's self-placement and for the respondent's placement of George Bush. The item continued with the same format for the placement of additional candidates and for the placement of parties.

Here is a seven-point scale on which the political views that people might hold are arranged from extremely liberal to extremely conservative. Where would you place yourself and each of the others listed on this scale?

		Extremely Liberal 1	Liberal 2	Slightly Liberal 3	Moderate Middle of road 4	Slightly Conservative 5	Conservative 6	Extremely Conservative 7
I don't know ☐	Yourself	☐	☐	☐	☐	☐	☐	☐
☐	George Bush	☐	☐	☐	☐	☐	☐	☐

Continuing the same format, respondents were asked to place Michael Dukakis, the Democratic party, the Republican party, Lloyd Bentsen, and Dan Quayle. Respondents who were sampled as giving to a Democratic candidate were asked to place the other five Democratic presidential candidates; respondents who were sampled as giving to a Republican candidate were asked to place the other four Republican candidates. Further, respondents were asked to recall the names of their House members and senators and candidates for those offices, and to place these individuals as well. Using an identically labeled liberal- conservative scale, the respondents were asked to place themselves on three more scales:

economic issues, involving taxing and spending decisions
defense issues, involving our relationship with Russia, aid to the contras, Star Wars and spending on our conventional and nuclear forces
social issues, such as abortion, mandatory school prayer, the death penalty, pornogaphy and so forth.

In addition respondents were asked six seven- point questions with labeled end points. The text of the first item was as follows:

Some people think the government should provide much less money for defense. Suppose these people are at one end of the scale at point 1. Other people feel that defense spending should be greatly increased. Suppose these people are at the other end, at point 7. And of course, some people have opinions somewhere in between. Where would you place yourself?

The remaining five items were asked in the same format as the one shown above:

- Some people value freedom above all other social values, while others value an ordered society.
- Some people feel the government in Washington should see to it that every person has a job and a good standard of living. Others think the government should just let each person get ahead on his own.
- Some people feel it is important for us to try to cooperate more with Russia, while others believe we should be much tougher in our dealings with Russia.
- Some people feel that the government in Washington should make every effort to improve the social and economic position of blacks. Others feel that the government should not make any special effort to help blacks because they should help themselves.
- Some people feel that women should have an equal role with men in running business, industry, and government. Others feel that women's place is in the home.

Economic competition items

In a third set of items, respondents were asked how strongly they favored or opposed each of the following measures designed to strengthen America's global economic position against Japan, Europe, and our other competitors. They were asked to indicate their level of support or opposition to the measure by rating it on a scale from 1 to 7, with 1 meaning the strongest opposition, 7 the strongest support, and 4 not caring one way or the other about the measure. The following were asked:

- Retaliatory tariffs and quotas against countries that bloc access of American goods to their markets.
- Tax breaks for businesses to encourage investment.
- A greatly expanded federal role in making sure our schools are as good as those of our economic competitors.
- Government subsidies to important industries threatened by overseas competitors.
- Limits to overseas investment in America.
- Cutting taxes and reducing interest rates to spur economic growth.
- Economic planning and targeting similar to that done in Japan.
- Requiring closer cooperation between business, labor and government in setting and carrying out economic agendas.
- Much stricter regulation of junk bonds, leveraged buyouts, hostile takeovers, and other Wall Street practices.
- Major increases in taxes to balance the federal budget.
- Major cuts in federal spending to balance the budget, even if it means cuts in things like Social Security, Medicare, and defense.
- Less regulation of industry including less environmental regulation.
- More federal support for science, research and development.
- Make Europe and Japan shoulder more of the defense burden.

Thermometer scales

Respondents were asked to rate candidates and organizations in terms of how favorably or unfavorably they felt toward them. They were told to use a scale between 0 and 100:

Ratings over 50 mean that you feel favorable toward that person. Ratings under 50 mean that you feel unfavorable. A rating of 50 indicates that you don't feel favorable or unfavorable but have some knowledge of the candidate. IF YOU HAVE NO KNOWLEDGE OF THE CANDIDATE OR NO OPINION ABOUT THE CANDIDATE PLEASE PLACE AN X ON THE LINE.

Respondents were asked to rate the following candidates:

Babbitt, Bentsen, Bush, Dole, Dukakis, du Pont, Gephardt, Gore, Jackson, Kemp, Quayle, Robertson, Simon.

They were also asked to provide the names of their House members and senators and to rate them.

They were asked to rate the following groups or organizations:

labor unions, big business, National Rifle Association, Republican party, Democratic party, civil rights leaders, liberals, conservatives, ACLU, feminists, moral majority, and the Supreme Court.

Contribution Items

Respondents were asked how frequently they had contributed money to presidential candidates. They were given the following options:

In most elections, in some elections, in one election, and never.

They were asked the same question for each of the following:

U.S. Senate candidates, U.S. House candidates, local candidates, political parties, and political action committees.

Respondents were asked which presidential candidates they contributed to in 1987–88, and how many contributions they made. Respondents were provided with a list of candidates and asked to check a yes box or a no box for each candidate. If they checked yes, they were asked to indicate the number of contributions.

Respondents were asked the following items with regard to the 1988 election:

• Did you solicit contributions from others for one of the presidential candidates yourself? Yes or No

- To how many political action committees (or PACs) did you contribute in 1987–1988? None, One, Two, or Three or more
- Did you contribute to either of the major parties directly in 1987–1988? Yes or No
- In how many Senate races did you contribute in 1987–1988? None, One, Two, or Three or more
- In how many House races did you contribute in 1987–1988? None, One, Two, or Three or more
- Did you make contributions to races:

In your own district	Yes or No
In your own state,but outside your district	Yes or No
In other states	Yes or No

- Which best characterizes the pattern of your contributions to candidates at all levels of office in the last 5 years:
    I contribute about equally to candidates of both major parties.
    I mostly contribute to candidates of one major party but occasionally give to candidates of the other party.
    I always give to candidates of the same party.
- Thinking back to when you made your first contribution to a presidential candidate in the recent election, how was that contribution solicited?
    I was asked by someone I knew personally.
    I was asked by someone I did not know personally.
    I received a request in the mail from someone I knew personally.
    I received a request in the mail from someone I did not know personally.

Other political participation and attitudinal items

Party identification
Respondents were asked if they generally thought of themselves as a:

strong Democrat; not very strong Democrat; Independent, closer to Democrat; Independent, closer to neither; Independent, closer to Republican; not very strong Republican; or strong Republican.

Respondents were asked to describe the importance of each of the following reasons for being active in politics. They were asked to describe the importance for them personally as very important, somewhat important, or not very important.

- Personal friendship for a candidate.
- My activity is a way of influencing policies of government.
- It is expected of someone in my position.
- Enjoyment of the friendships and social contacts.
- Political activity gives me a feeling of recognition.
- My activity helps me fulfill my sense of community obligation.
- My participation might really make a difference in the outcome of an election.

• For business or employment reasons

Respondents were asked if they had ever done anything to try to influence an act of Congress. They were asked to mark all the following that applied.

• Never tried to influence an act of Congress.
• I have worked through informal groups; talked to friends and neighbors to get them to take action.
• I have worked through a political party.
• I have worked through formal groups other than parties.
• I have, as an individual, written or telegrammed Senators, Congressmen or the President.
• I have, as an individual, spoken with a staff member of a Senator, Congressman or the President.
• I have taken part in a demonstration or other visible form of protest.

Respondents were asked if they had held any of the following sorts of offices at any level of government.

• *Political party positions,* such as state committee member, county chairperson, etc.
• *Public elective office,* such as state senator, council member, etc.
• *Public appointive office,* such as zoning board member, state commissioner, etc.

Respondents were asked how they voted in the last four presidential elections. For each election the options given were:

Republican candidate by name; Democratic candidate by name; other candidate; I did not vote; I don't remember.

Respondents were asked how frequently they had worked for presidential candidates, and given the example of whether they had canvassed a precinct or organized a rally. They were given the following options:

In most elections; in some elections; in one election; never.

They were asked the same question for each of the following:

U.S. Senate candidates, U.S. House candidates, local candidates, political parties, and political action committees.

Respondents were asked if they had ever taken part in forming a new group or a new organization to try to solve some community problem.

Demographics

The following items were asked:

• What is your sex? Male Female
• What is the year of your birth? _____
• How many years of education did you complete?
        Grade school or less (0–8 years)
        High school (8–12 years)
        Some college
        College graduate
        Some graduate school
        Master's degree; M.D., Ph.D., LL.B., and so forth
• If you do not mind answering, what is your race?
        White, Black, Asian, or Other
• What was your approximate family income last year – before taxes?
        Under 25,000
        25,000 to 49,999
        50,000 to 99,999
        100,000 to 249,999
        250,000 and over
        I prefer not to answer
• What is your religious denomination? (PLEASE BE SPECIFIC)
  Please check all the terms that accurately reflect your religious beliefs.

Fundamentalist Christian	Mainline Christian
Evangelical Christian	Liberal Christian
Born again Christian	Ethical humanist
Conservative Christian	Religious non Christian
Charismatic Christian	No religion, agnostic or atheist

        None of these terms

1992 SURVEY ITEMS USED IN ANALYSIS

Thermometer scores

These were asked for the 1992 presidential candidates.

Contribution Items

Three sets of items measured patterns of contribution and solicitation:

When you made your first contribution to any of the presidential nomination candidates below in this election (if you made a contribution), please indicate the method by which that contribution was sought. Please check one box for each candidate:

For each 1992 presidential candidate the following options were provided:

• I did not contribute to this candidate.
• I was asked in person or on the phone by someone I knew personally.
• I received a request in the mail from someone I knew personally.
• I was asked in person or on the phone by someone I did not know personally.
• I received a request in the mail from someone I did not know personally.
• I responded to a TV, radio, or newspaper appeal.

On any occasion when you were asked and declined to make a contribution to a presidential candidate in this election (whether or not you gave to that candidate on a different occasion), how were you asked? Please check as many boxes as apply for each candidate:

For each candidate the following options were provided:

• I was asked in person or on the phone by someone I knew personally.
• I received a request in the mail from someone I knew personally.
• I was asked in person or on the phone by someone I did not know personally.
• I received a request in the mail from someone I did not know personally.
• I was not asked by any of these means.

If you made a contribution of any size to the campaign of a presidential nomination candidate in this election, to which of the following candidates did you contribute, and, if you do not mind answering, approximately how many different contributions did you make, and how much money did you contribute? A list of candidates and answer options followed.

In addition, respondents were asked the following items for the 1992 presidential nomination election cycles:

• Were you asked to solicit contributions from others for one of the presidential candidates either year? Yes or No
• Did you yourself in fact solicit contributions from others for one of the presidential candidates in either year?
• If you solicited contributions from others, approximately how many people did you ask to make a contribution to a presidential nomination candidate?
• To the best of your knowledge, how many people that you asked to contribute actually did contribute to a presidential nomination candidate in each election?

Attitudinal Items

Respondents were asked to rate their own liberalism–conservatism and that of the 1992 candidates as they were in 1988.

• How would you rate the job that George Bush is doing as President?
    Excellent
    Very good
    Poor
    Very poor

If you did not make a contribution to a presidential candidate in this election, or if you contributed substantially less than you did in the last presidential nomination campaign, please describe the importance of each of the following reasons for not making a contribution or for contributing less. Respondents were given choices of: very important; somewhat important; not very important.

• I was not asked.
• No candidate seemed well- qualified to be president.
• No candidate represented my views.
• I felt that no candidate I supported had a chance of winning.
• I had less money to commit to political activities this year.
• I saw little to be gained personally or professionally by contributing.
• I don't enjoy as much as I used to the friendships and social contacts that go with contributing.
• I was generally disgusted by the nature of the campaign this year.
• I was not under any business pressure to contribute.
• No one I knew personally asked me to contribute.

Demographics

Which of the following best describes your occupation?

• Business/financial owner, manager, executive
• Professional (doctor, lawyer, teacher, accountant, etc.)
• "Lobbyist," DC representative for industry or profession, etc.
• Independent contractor (real estate agent, consultant, etc.)
• White collar employer (clerical, sales, etc.)
• Blue collar worker
• Retired
• At home

Notes

Chapter 1

1. Even so, among Democrats the candidate who spent the most on Super Tuesday won in 75% of the states, and in all but one of the other states, the biggest spender finished second to Jackson.
2. Indeed, in a related matter, some research suggests that spending may not help congressional incumbents increase their vote (Jacobson 1980, 1990; but see also Bartels 1991; Green and Krasno 1988, 1990).
3. Wilcox (1991, p. 101). In previous elections, candidates who won in Iowa or New Hampshire got a "bump" in fundraising, in part because the victories established viability, created bandwagons, and gave positive publicity to the candidate. In 1984, for example, Hart got a real bump in individual contributions after his New Hampshire victory (Orren 1985), and was able to borrow even more money against future matching funds from this flood of contributions.
4. See Malbin (1985, p. 74).
5. Interview with Terry McAuliffe, October 15, 1992.
6. Interview, September 19, 1992.
7. Ibid.
8. Frank Sorauf (1988) estimated that 800,000 individuals made contributions to presidential candidates in 1984, arguing that the number of individuals who made multiple contributions were balanced by the number who gave anonymously or who gave to candidates who did not qualify for matching funds. Our survey suggests that contributors of more than $200 to a single candidate in 1988 gave an average of approximately 2 contributions apiece that appeared on the FEC lists. There were 1,245,501 contributions submitted for matching during the 1988 election cycle. The contributors of serious money are, of course, a subset of all contributors described by Sorauf. The 1992 estimate is ours, based on FEC data.
9. We do not include contributors to Alexander Haig, Joe Biden, or Gary Hart, who left the campaign early. We do include Bruce Babbitt, who raised more money than those three candidates but also left the campaign early. See Appendix I for more details about this survey.
10. Since this survey was to look at what the 1988 pool did in 1992, the cases for 1992 were assigned the same weights as for 1988.
11. The 1972 disclosure laws took effect on April 4, 1972, in midseason. The population surveyed was those who contributed after this date. Although contributions

made before this date were probably larger than those made after the date, since there was no limit on the size of a contribution and multiple contributions were encouraged, it is highly probable that a very large percentage of those who contributed before April 4 also contributed afterward.

12. This survey was conducted by Clifford W. Brown, Lynda W. Powell, and Roman B. Hedges. For the details of the survey, see Brown, Hedges, and Powell (1980a).

Chapter 2

1. Individuals can give no more than $20,000 to political parties, no more than $5,000 to political action committees (PACs), and no more than $5,000 to any single party committee. Individuals are also limited to a sum of $25,000 in total contributions to candidates, parties, and PACs during an election cycle.

2. There are other sources of cash for campaigns. Candidates are allowed to borrow money to finance their campaigns, as long as the transaction is truly a loan. To ensure that it is, creditors are not permitted to forgive any loan in excess of $1,000. Candidates are permitted to transfer funds into their campaign committees without restriction from Senate and House campaign committees. They can also transfer funds from gubernatorial or other campaign committees as long as these funds were raised in ways consistent with the rules governing contributions to presidential nomination candidates. Such transfers have not played a large role in the past but may be potential features of home-state financial bases in the future.

3. Many presidential hopefuls form PACs or foundations that have the development and honing of donor lists as one of their major purposes, although these activities are not evident from the reports of their campaign committees (Corrado 1992). These PACs also allow candidates to avoid the limits on individual contributions: supporters can contribute up to $5,000 to the potential candidate's PAC, and after the formation of an official campaign committee they can contribute an additional $1,000 to that committee. Although no comprehensive information is available on the extent of double contributions, a Washington Post analysis suggested that in the first part of 1987 alone, 76 individuals contributed both to George Bush's PAC and to his campaign committee, and 79 gave to the PAC and campaign committee of Robert Dole. These double givers gave an average of nearly $5,000 to the Bush committees, and just over $4,000 to the Dole efforts (Morin 1988). Undoubtedly a more complete study of double contributions, including contributions to presidential PACs as early as 1985 and contributions to campaign committees through the 1988 primaries, would turn up many more examples.

4. John Connally in 1980 chose not to accept matching funds, but his campaign floundered, and he won only one pledged delegate.

5. Cited in May (1987).

6. We have calculated this on the basis of all receipts through May 31, 1988.

7. Interview with Roger Craver, October 15, 1992.

8. Alexander (1979, p. 262).

9. Babcock and Morin (1988a, p. A4).
10. Werth (1988, p. 39).
11. Half the money contributed in amounts of $500 or more came from just five states in 1988: New York, California, Texas, Florida, and Massachusetts. And, although Jackson and Robertson relied primarily on direct mail solicitation, half of Jackson's $500 and larger contributions came from New York and California, and half of Robertson's came from Texas, California, and Florida. Compare these results with those in Alexander (1976, chapter 11).
12. Babbitt borrowed in late 1987; Gore's campaign borrowed approximately $1 million before the Super Tuesday primaries, mostly using future matching funds as collateral (Runkel 1989).

Chapter 3

1. It is illegal, however, to use the FEC-generated list of contributors of serious money, and this list is "seeded" with fake names to catch fundraisers who violate the law by attempting to use it.
2. Recall that we have weighted these data to compensate for the larger probability of selecting those whose names appear on lists for more than one candidate.
3. When we present candidate differences in the analysis that follows, we need a way to treat those respondents who gave to more than one candidate. In order to be confident that we have a representative sample of contributors to each candidate, we have coded these multiple givers as giving to the candidate from whose records we sampled their name.
4. Contributors were asked how frequently they gave to candidates at several levels of government and to parties, and also if they had made such a contribution in 1988. From these results we could quantify what contributors meant when they said they gave in "most" or in "some" elections. For example, 81% of those who say they give in most elections to Senate candidates gave to Senate candidates in 1988; 83% of those who give in most elections to House candidates did so in 1988; and 88% of those who give to parties in most elections gave in 1988. From this we estimated what was meant by "most," and from a similar calculation what was meant by "some." For purposes of this estimate, we assumed that the likelihood of a first-time contributor making a contribution during the next cycle was the same as the likelihood of those who say they give in "some" elections.
5. There was no correlation between frequency of past giving and responding to the 1992 survey, so our estimate of 1992 giving is not contaminated by differential rates of survey response.
6. Among Democrats, no candidate approached Jackson's liberalism, even though Harkin tried to appeal both to Jackson's rainbow coalition and to Simon's labor base. Among the Republicans, only one strong conservative sought office, and Buchanan's foreign policy views were clearly different from those of Kemp, Robertson, and du Pont in 1988, perhaps preventing him from fully mobilizing their constituencies. In addition, his Catholicism may have prevented him from tapping seriously into Robertson's Pentecostal supporters.

7. Interestingly, the strongly liberal whites who gave to Jackson were much less likely to give again in 1992 than were his moderate black contributors.

8. By comparing the names of individuals in our survey with those that appeared on the computerized FEC lists of individuals who made a single contribution of more than $200 in the 1989–90 election cycle, we identified 32% giving to Senate candidates, 31% to House candidates, and 30% to parties. For several reasons these results understate the extent to which donors of serious money in the 1988 presidential cycle actually contributed serious money to federal candidates and to parties in the 1990 cycle. First, the FEC computerized list for 1990 omits those contributors of serious money whose contributions aggregated to $200, but who did not give that much at any one time. Second, we have adopted conservative rules to help us identify which contributions are made by the same individuals when the records differ slightly in the reporting of names or addresses. Furthermore, addresses may change, and, less often, names may change, typically through marriage. Finally, some of the contributors will be deceased or too ill to contribute in a subsequent election. Although the extent of our inability to locate all subsequent contributions cannot be estimated fully, we can give some indication of the magnitude of the problem by noting that a search of the 1987–88 computerized records for the contributions matching those of our respondents sampled for those years located only 84% of the names when most of the problems of matching cited above were absent. Conservatively, we may therefore assume that *at least* 36% to 38% of those who contributed serious money to a presidential candidate in 1988 also contributed serious money to a federal candidate or to a party in 1990.

9. The percentage who worked in no more than one election for each type of candidate or for a political party increased from 33% in 1972 to 42% in 1988.

10. There are some sharp differences across contributors to various candidates in their modes of participation. A majority of McGovern's contributors in 1972 and of Jackson's contributors in 1988 said they had participated in demonstrations; this was also true for a third of Simon's contributors. Generally, few Republican contributors had demonstrated, although nearly one in six of those who contributed to Robertson had done so. There are clear cleavages between those who contributed to establishment politicians and those who gave to the outsiders, especially Jackson and Robertson. Contributors to each of the latter were more likely to report working through informal groups than through the parties, were relatively less likely than other contributors to contact public officials directly, and were more likely to demonstrate.

11. By targeted solicitations we mean direct mail, telemarketing calls, personal solicitations, and other approaches directed specifically at the potential contributor, and not media appeals for funds.

12. Of course, it is possible that those who made small contributions to candidates and whose total gifts did not aggregate to more than $200 differ greatly from those whose donations pass the FEC disclosure threshold. The existence of federal matching funds encourages candidates to appeal to those who make smaller contributions, and who therefore do not show up in our sample. We are inclined to believe that those who give such small donations are similar to

those whose small gifts aggregate to $200, although our data do not allow us to demonstrate this.

13. Robertson's contributors were less educated and less affluent than Jackson's, in part because Jackson attracted financial support from wealthy and well-educated liberal whites. One in six of Robertson's contributors had family incomes less than $25,000, compared to just 6% for Jackson. One in six Robertson contributors had completed high school or less, compared with only 5% for Jackson.

14. Of course all contributors sampled made contributions that aggregated to over $200.

15. Celinda Lake, a public opinion and fundraising specialist, told us that her research suggests that women are more likely than men to consider a gift of a given amount as large, even after income is controlled. (Interview, September 1993.)

16. For some respondents, friendship for a candidate may merely indicate positive affect toward a political figure they have never met but admire, others may have met the candidate at a fundraising dinner, and still others may actually know the candidate personally.

17. We do think it likely that our survey data understate the importance of material motives. Survey respondents typically understate the importance of socially undesirable motivations and overstate the importance of socially desirable ones. Further, our interviews with campaign officials emphasize the importance of material motives in personal networks. This is a common problem in survey research and does not pose a difficulty for analysis that is based on making relative comparisons across groups within the sample. Our analysis is based on just such comparisons.

Chapter 4

1. List vendors generally "salt" the list with fake names to enable them to identify candidates who violate the rule of one solicitation per rental.

2. Hal Malchow, a direct mail expert who worked for Dukakis, Kerrey, and later Clinton, described to us how a California voter list was crossed with lists giving: three different indicators of family income, the number of household wage earners, the cash value of the home, the age of family members, the number of children, the make of car(s), shopping habits, and responsiveness to mail solicitation. (Interview, October 14, 1992.)

3. For example, some individuals sampled from Robertson's list gave several gifts a month, and occasionally several small gifts in a single week.

4. Interview with McKenzie, October 13, 1992.

5. Lists that produced a net gain before the match tended to include moderate and traditional liberal groups, while those that did not work (before the match) included more ideologically oriented groups.

6. Interview with Terry McAuliffe, the chief fundraiser for Gephardt in 1988, October 15, 1992; interview with Mike Berman, a fundraiser for Humphrey and Mondale, October 14, 1992. Phil Smith, a fundraiser for Ford in 1976 and director of finance at the RNC in the 1980s, estimates that there are 20 to 30 top

fundraisers among the Republicans, and that there are over 200 major solicitors that these fundraisers try to tap. (Interview, October 13, 1992.) Margaret Alexander, a major fundraiser for Bush in 1988 estimates that there are 300 to 400 major Republican solicitors. (Interview, October 15, 1992.)

7. One top fundraiser was cited to us as having been responsible for raising $2.5 million. Most top fundraisers, of course, cannot raise amounts this large.

8. Interview with Margaret Alexander, October 15, 1992.

9. Babcock and Morin (1988b, at p. A12).

10. Berke (1988c, at p. 20, column 3).

11. Werth (1988, p. 38).

12. Ibid, pp. 40–41.

13. Those involved in the labor movement do very little networking.

14. Werth (1988, p. 37).

15. Ibid, p. 39.

16. Berke (1988b).

17. Stark (1988), Section 3, p. 8.

18. This leads to many different personal styles of operation. Compare Berke (1988a), Brownstein (1987, section 6, p. 46), and Dowd (1987).

19. Berke (1988b). See also Werth (1988, p. 44, "Mann," and pp. 45–46, "Borman").

20. Nearly 20% of those who gave to Robertson indicated that they had been contacted by mail by someone they knew, and Richard Weingold of the Robertson campaign assured us that nearly all fundraising letters went out over Robertson's signature. It seems unlikely that one in five of Robertson's many contributors knew him personally, but nearly all had regularly watched his television show. This daily contact in the privacy of their living rooms may have persuaded many respondents that they in fact "knew" Robertson.

21. Although a telemarketing contact may seem to be a form of personal contact, it is only artificially personalized and is fundamentally different from a personal contact by an acquaintance.

22. Interestingly, those solicited by mail by a personal acquaintance were especially likely to be party or appointed officials. Bush, Gephardt, and to a lesser extent Gore appear to have mailed to local party and appointed officials.

23. To measure agreement in partisanship, a contributor was counted as giving in agreement if he or she was sampled as giving to a candidate of the same party. A contributor was counted as being in disagreement if partisanship did not match. No score was given if the contributor identified him- or herself as an independent with no party leaning or if the contributor did not indicate a party preference. To measure agreement on ideology, a contributor was counted as being in agreement if he or she placed the candidate and him- or herself on the same side of the scale. That is, both were placed as liberals or both as conservatives, though there may have been some difference in how liberal or how conservative they were. If either the contributor placed himself or herself or the candidate in the middle or did not provide a placement for either, no score was given. In addition to the results presented in the text, 19.8% matched on one dimension and had no score on the other, 3.6% were unscored on both dimensions, 4.5% matched on one dimension and conflicted on the other, and 3.1% conflicted on one dimension and had no score on the other.

Chapter 5

1. Our data do not contain sufficient numbers of contributors to several of the candidates to analyze early home-state fundraising efforts.
2. The most notable exception is Jesse Jackson, who, we estimate, received 16% of his serious money from Illinois, although only 5% of his gifts of $500 or more came from in-state.
3. Although these figures show the number of contributors, not contribution totals, the average size of these donations in-state and out-of-state were not significantly different.
4. Kemp increased his money from New York City in this later period, but the percentage of money from his congressional district declined after the first period.
5. We obtain very similar results if we use the number of top wealth holders in a state divided by the number of $500 contributions and up.
6. Kemp raised approximately one-third of his in-state early gifts of $500 or more from Buffalo, not including the suburbs and rural areas of his district. Overall, however, his statewide yield was quite low. In a state as large and diverse as New York, an upstate district far removed from New York City is unlikely to provide a good starting point to establish a statewide base of support, although he raised almost as much early money from New York City as he did from Buffalo. Although Kemp·relied on New York money to a considerable extent, he received only 16% of the early Republican money in New York. Both Bush and Dole received more early money from New York than Kemp. This analysis was done using ZIP codes for each contributor. We used only ZIP codes for the cities of St. Louis, Buffalo, and New York. Obviously, substantial numbers of contributors from the suburban areas of these cities would also have contributed, but had different ZIP codes. The New York case is probably the most difficult, for many commuters live outside of New York State. The figures cited therefore understate the amount of in-district money for Kemp and Gephardt.
7. We used only those ZIP codes for the metropolitan areas in this analysis.
8. Thanks to Robert Biersack for help with this analysis. The lower threshold resulted in somewhat depressed percentages, for in-state early gifts were larger on average than out-of-state early gifts. For example, Kerrey raised 23% of his contributions of over $200 from his home state, but 29% of gifts of $500 or more.
9. We have sufficient numbers of cases to make reasonable claims about the national networks of Bush ($n = 156$), Dole ($n = 71$), and Dukakis ($n = 110$). The number of respondents who were solicited through national networks for Gephardt ($n = 30$), Gore ($n = 46$) and Simon ($n = 24$) are too small for confident conclusions, yet we include a description of their networks in the discussion below because the results neatly fit with what we were told by fundraising professionals.
10. Most of these Republicans who gave to Gore or Gephardt reported voting for Republican presidential candidates in all elections since 1976, including 1988. Many did not give to any candidate in 1992, but among those who did, nearly two-thirds gave to another Democrat, usually Clinton. This suggests that there may be a network of Republican business leaders in the South who are regularly solicited by, and give to, Democratic candidates.

11. Many of these solicitors were lobbyist/lawyers, who form an important part of Senate fundraising efforts.

12. Approximately a third of those who gave to Robertson's national network attended pentecostal churches, compared with about one in six contributors solicited other than through a national network. It should be noted that a substantial majority of Robertson's contributors identified themselves as charismatics. The latter term indicates a style of worship filled with imminent expressions of the Holy Spirit – a worship style sometimes found in mainline Protestant and even Catholic churches, while the pentecostal label refers to specific denominations such as the Assemblies of God.

13. Buchanan and Bush both solicited Robertson's charismatic network in 1992, and approximately a third did not contribute, a third gave to Bush, and a third gave to Buchanan.

14. Private communication.

15. Although we do not present data from 1992 in Table 5.6, fully 76% of those who gave to Bush rated Buchanan as extremely conservative, as did 48% of those who gave to Buchanan. Nearly 6 in 10 of those who gave to other Democratic candidates rated Brown as extremely liberal, as did half of those who gave to his campaign. Approximately a quarter of those who gave to other Democratic candidates rated Harkin as extreme, as did 16% of those who gave to his campaign. That Brown, who championed a flat income tax, was rated as extremely liberal by a majority of Democratic contributors in 1992, is noteworthy.

16. Of course, it is important to remember that our measure of ideology for Dukakis is contaminated by the ideological nature of the 1988 campaign. The first wave of our survey was mailed soon after an election in which Bush frequently accused Dukakis of being an extreme liberal, and in which Dukakis did not mount a satisfactory retort.

17. Simon was also able to build a party network, both in his home state and nationally. Further, his campaign was relatively short and was based essentially on seed money, which is often raised through a personal network.

18. The same argument applies as well to primary election voters, however.

19. Of course, those who made several contributions that aggregated to more than $200 may be different in some ways from those who gave a single small gift. Our data do not allow us to examine these differences.

20. Each item was normalized and averaged within a policy area. The same method was used for the economic competitiveness items discussed immediately below.

21. Purposive motives dominated the equation, but solidary motives were also positive and achieved statistical significance. Contributors who were low on material motives were also significantly more likely to give to the most ideologically proximate candidate.

22. We do not include the issue divisions in 1992 because we do not have a sample of the new contributors to any candidate. For example, the Buchanan contributors in our survey are only those who gave to Kemp, Robertson, or some other candidate in 1988, and we do not have those new contributors whom Buchanan brought into the pool. In 1988, the new Robertson contributors were not ideologically different

from those who had given in previous elections, but we prefer to be cautious in inferring the ideological nature of candidate coalitions.

23. Individuals differ in their responses to feeling thermometers, and in mass samples it is frequently necessary to adjust these measures for individual differences (Wilcox, Sigelman, and Cook 1989). In this elite sample, however, the high level of attitudinal constraint means that there is no real difference in the results when these scores are adjusted. For ease of presentation, we therefore present the unadjusted scores.

24. For a similar result using mass survey data, see Wilcox (1992).

25. The obvious exception is the organized efforts of labor groups on behalf of Walter Mondale in 1984.

26. Although multinomial logit is currently the statistic of choice for this sort of analysis, our independent variables are highly correlated. Discriminant analysis allows us to include these variables, and groups them into canonical functions that help to distinguish between those who gave to each candidate.

Chapter 6

1. Of course, the 1988 contributor pool is still a subset of a larger pool of presidential nomination contributors of serious money, and we cannot argue that our sample is fully representative of this larger pool. However, because the 1988 campaign included candidates in both parties representing a wide range of ideological positions, our sample from that year is probably more representative of the pool than would have been the case in any other presidential election conducted under current campaign finance rules. Moreover, since our focus is on individual decisions rather than on a descriptive profile of the 1992 contributors, this does not pose a serious problem for analysis.

2. Since each equation predicts the number of campaigns that approached each contributor using a given method, each contributor appears once in each equation. If a contributor was solicited by two different campaigns by mail and not solicited through personal networks, they have a value of 2 in the mail equation and a value of 0 in the network equation. Contributors solicited once by each method have values of 1 for each equation.

3. Our data show that Bush solicited approximately 90% of those who gave to his campaign in 1988 and who responded to our 1992 survey. We think that it is likely that Bush in fact solicited 100%, which suggests an error rate of around 10%. Because the question asks respondents to recall solicitations by candidates several months earlier, this is a surprisingly low error rate.

4. In making this estimate, we calculate the predicted probability of contributing based on the logistic regression, setting all cases first to the moderate category of the extremism scale, and then to the extreme category. We hold constant the values of all the other variables at their sample distributions in making the estimation. This same procedure is used for all subsequent estimates.

5. Of course, it is quite possible that even this is response error.

6. That is to say, the predictive ability of the equation is significantly improved by adding these two variables together as a bloc.

7. In the subsequent section sample sizes are quite modest because we are looking at only those who were asked to solicit. In that analysis, we were especially interested in maximizing sample size. We treated income as a series of dichotomous dummy variables, allowing us to include those who did not reveal their income as a category. For consistency, we followed the same procedure in this section as well.

8. Unfortunately we cannot examine ideological congruence with the candidate, which we found to be intertwined with the purposive motive in contribution decisions. Limits of questionnaire space precluded asking which candidate asked the individual to solicit.

Bibliography

Abramowitz, Alan I., 1989. "Viability, Electability, and Candidate Choice in a Presidential Primary Election: A Test of Competing Models." *Journal of Politics*, 51, 977–92.

Abramson, Paul R., John H. Aldrich, and David W. Rhode, 1990. *Change and Continuity in the 1988 Elections.* Washington, D.C.: CQ Press.

Adamany, David W., and George E. Agee, 1975. *Political Money.* Baltimore: Johns Hopkins University Press.

Aldrich, John, 1980. *Before the Convention: Strategies and Choices in Presidential Nominating Campaigns.* Chicago: University of Chicago Press.

Alexander, Herbert, 1971. *Financing the 1968 Election.* Lexington, Mass.: Heath Lexington Books.

1976. *Financing the 1972 Election.* Lexington, Mass.: Lexington Books.

1979. *Financing the 1976 Election.* Washington, D.C.: CQ Press.

1983. *Financing the 1980 Election.* Lexington, Mass.: Lexington Books.

1984. *Financing Politics*, 3d edition. Washington, D.C.: CQ Press.

1987. *Financing the 1984 Election.* Lexington, Mass.: D. C. Heath.

1989. "American Presidential Elections Since Public Funding, 1976–84." In Herbert Alexander (ed.), *Comparative Political Finance in the 1980s.* Cambridge: Cambridge University Press.

1991. *Reform and Reality: The Financing of State and Local Campaigns.* New York: Twentieth Century Fund Press.

Alexander, Herbert, and Monica Bauer, 1991. *Financing the 1988 Election.* Boulder, Colo.: Westview.

Alexander, Herbert, and Anthony Corrado, 1994. *Financing the 1992 Election.* Armonk, N.Y.: M.E. Sharpe.

Alexander, Herbert, and Brian Haggerty, 1981. *The Federal Election Campaign Act After a Decade of Political Reform.* Los Angeles: Citizen's Research Foundation.

Arnold, Douglas R., 1990. *The Logic of Congressional Action.* New Haven: Yale University Press.

Babcock, Charles, 1992. "Both Parties Raise Millions in 'Soft Money.'" *Washington Post*, July 26, A1.

Babcock, Charles R., and Richard Morin, 1988a. "Bush's Money Machine: Cadre of Friends Help Raise $29 Million." *Washington Post*, May 15, 1988, A1.

1988b. "Greek Americans, Home State Boost Dukakis' Coffers." *Washington Post*, May 29, 1988, A1.

Baida, Peter, 1992. "The Legacy of Dollar Mark Hanna." In Stephen J. Wayne and

Clyde Wilcox (eds.), *The Quest for National Office*. New York: St. Martin's.

Barber, James David, ed., 1978. *Race for the Presidency: The Media and the Nominating Process*. Englewood Cliffs, N.J.: Prentice Hall.

Bartels, Larry M., 1988. *Presidential Primaries and the Dynamics of Public Choice*. Princeton, N.J.: Princeton University Press.

1991. "Instrumental and 'Quasi-Instrumental' Variables." *American Journal of Political Science*, 35, 777–800.

Bendyna, Mary E., and Celinda C. Lake, 1994. "Gender and Voting in the 1972 Presidential Election." In Elizabeth Adell Cook, Sue Thomas, and Clyde Wilcox (eds.), *The Year of the Woman: Myths and Realities*. Boulder, Colo.: Westview.

Berg, Larry, Larry Eastland, and Sherry Bebitch Jaffe, 1981. "Characteristics of Large Campaign Contributors." *Social Science Quarterly*, 62, 409–23.

Berke, Richard, 1987a. "New Light Shed on Murky World of Campaign Fund Raising by Executives." *New York Times*, December 7, A28.

1987b. "Heeding Plato, Greek Americans Aid in Effort to Raise Money for Dukakis." *New York Times*, December 27, A20.

1988a. "Mastermind of the Dukakis Success." *New York Times*, March 21, B6.

1988b. "The Ideal Fund–Raiser: Vocal, Aware and Rich." *New York Times*, April 15, A21.

1988c. "Fund–Raisers Give Dukakis a Huge Edge." *New York Times*, May 22, Section 1, 1.

1988d. "Candidates and Stars Bask in Mutual Spotlight." *New York Times*, June 5, A24.

Biersack, Robert, Clifford Brown, Paul Herrnson, Lynda Powell, and Clyde Wilcox, 1992. "Seeking the Source of the Money Stream: The Flow of Individual Contributions in Federal Elections." Paper given at the annual meeting of The Midwest Political Science Association, Chicago.

Biersack, Robert, Paul S. Herrnson, Wesley Joe, and Clyde Wilcox, 1994. "Individual Contributors in Congressional Elections: A Preliminary Investigation." Paper presented at the annual meeting of the Midwest Political Science Association, Chicago.

Biersack, Robert, Paul S. Herrnson, and Clyde Wilcox, 1993. "Seeds for Success: Early Money in Congressional Elections." *Legislative Studies Quarterly*, 18, 535–52.

Biersack, Robert, Paul S. Herrnson, and Clyde Wilcox, eds., 1994. *Risky Business? PAC Decisionmaking in Congressional Elections*. Armonk, N.Y.: M.E. Sharpe.

Biersack, Robert, and Clyde Wilcox, 1990. "Financing National Campaigns: A Research Agenda." *American Politics Quarterly*, 18, 215–41.

Blow, Richard, 1988. "Rolling in It." *New Republic*, March 21, 40.

Blumenthal, Sidney, 1980. *The Permanant Campaign: Inside the World of Elite Political Operatives*. Boston: Beacon Press.

1990. *Pledging Allegiance*. New York: HarperCollins.

Boyce, Katharine, and Richard Messick, 1988. "Don't Contribute to Campaign-Law Trouble." *Wall Street Journal*, February 22, 20.

Brown, Clifford, Roman Hedges, and Lynda Powell, 1980a. "Modes of Elite Political Participation: Contributors to the 1972 Presidential Candidates." *American Journal of Political Science*, 24, 259–90.

1980b. "Belief Structure in a Political Elite: Contributors to the 1972 Presidential Candidates." *Polity,* 8, 134–46.

Brown, Clifford, Lynda Powell, and Clyde Wilcox, 1990a. "The Constituency Base of Campaign Contributions to the 1988 Presidential Nomination Candidates: A Preliminary Analysis." Paper given at the annual meeting of the American Political Science Association, San Francisco.

1990b. "The Ideological Base of Presidential Pre-Nomination Fundraising." Paper given at the Southern Political Science Association Meetings, Atlanta.

1990c. "Personal and Impersonal Means of First Solicitation in Presidential Nomination Campaigns: A Preliminary Analysis." Paper given at the Northeast Political Science Association Meetings, Providence.

1991a. "Serious Money: Presidential Campaign Contributors and Patterns of Contributions in 1988." In Stephen J. Wayne and Clyde Wilcox (eds.), *The Quest For Office: National Electoral Politics.* New York: St. Martin's.

1991b. "Solicitors of Money for 1988 Presidential Nomination Candidates." Paper given at the annual meeting of The American Political Science Association, Washington, D.C.

1991c. "National Networks in Presidential Fundraising." Paper given at the Southern Political Science Association Meeting, Tampa, Fla.

Brownstein, Ronald, 1986. "Getting an Early Start." *National Journal,* November 29, 2876–81.

1987. "Raising Bucks for Bush." *New York Times,* May 17, Section 6, 42.

1990. *The Power and the Glitter: The Hollywood-Washington Connection.* New York: Pantheon.

1991. "Have Mouth, Will Travel." *National Journal,* January 5, 3.

Buchanan, Bruce, 1991. *Electing a President: The Markle Commission Report on Campaign '88.* Austin: University of Texas Press.

Cain, Bruce E., I. A. Lewis, and Douglas Rivers, 1989. "Strategy and Choice in the 1988 Presidential Primaries." *Electoral Studies* 8, 23–48.

Cesar, James W., 1979. *Presidential Selection: Theory and Development.* Princeton: Princeton University Press.

1982. *Reforming the Reforms: A Critical Analysis of the Presidential Selection Process.* Cambridge, Mass.: Ballinger.

Clausen, Aage R., 1973. *How Congressmen Decide: A Policy Focus.* New York: St. Martin's.

Clawson, Dan, Alan Neustadtl, and James Bearden, 1986. "The Logic of Business Unity: Corporate Contributions to the 1980 Congressional Elections." *American Sociological Review,* 51, 797–811.

Congressional Quarterly Weekly Report, 1992. "Tsongas Suspends Campaign." March 21, 749.

Conover, Pamela J., and Stanley Feldman, 1981. "The Origins and Meaning of Liberal/Conservative Self-Identifications." *American Journal of Political Science,* 25, 617–45.

Converse, Philip. E., 1964. "The Nature of Belief Systems in Mass Publics." In David Apter (ed.), *Ideology and Discontent.* New York: Free Press.

Constantini, Edmond, and Joel King, 1982. "Checkbook Democrats and Their

Copartisans: Campaign Contributors and California Political Leaders, 1964–1976." *American Politics Quarterly*, 10, 65–92.

Cook, Elizabeth Adell, 1994. "Voter Responses to Women Senate Candidates." In Elizabeth Adell Cook, Sue Thomas, and Clyde Wilcox (eds.), *The Year of the Woman : Myths and Realities*. Boulder, Colo.: Westview.

Cook, Elizabeth Adell, Ted G. Jelen, and Clyde Wilcox, 1992. *Between Two Absolutes: Public Opinion and the Politics of Abortion*. Boulder, Colo.: Westview.

Cook, Rhodes, 1986. "In '88 Contest, It's What's Up Front That Counts." *Congressional Quarterly Weekly Report*, August 23, 1997–2002.

    1989. "The Nominating Process." In M. Nelson (ed.), *The Elections of 1988*. Washington, D.C.: CQ Press.

Corrado, Anthony, 1992. *Creative Financing*. Boulder, Colo.: Westview.

Cotter, Cornelius, James Gibson, John Bibby, and Robert Huckshorn, 1984. *Party Organization in American Politics*. New York: Praeger.

Crotty, William, and John S. Jackson, III, 1985. *Presidential Primaries and Nominations*. Washington, D.C.: CQ Press.

Crotty, William J., and Gary C. Jacobson, 1980. *American Parties in Decline*. Boston: Little, Brown.

Devroy, Ann, and Charles Babcock, 1992. "GOP Dinner Criticized as Symptom of System." *Washington Post*, April 24, A1.

Devroy, Ann, and Mark Stencel, 1992. "Bush Dinner Raises Funds and Eyebrows." *Washington Post*, April 16, A1.

Dowd, Maureen, 1987. "Money for Politics: One Man's Relentless Pursuit." *New York Times*, July 7, A12.

Drew, Elizabeth, 1977. *American Journal: The Events of 1976*. New York: Random House.

    1983. *Politics and Money*. New York: Macmillan.

Dunn, Delmer, 1965. "Policy Preferences of Party Contributors and Voters." *Social Science Quarterly*, 55, 983–90.

    1972. *Financing Presidential Campaigns*. Washington, D.C.: Brookings.

    1974. "Contributors in the American Electoral Process." *American Politics Quarterly*, 2, 221–30.

Dutton, Frederick G., 1971. *Changing Sources of Power*. New York: McGraw-Hill.

Eichel, Larry, 1989. "Money and the Campaign." In David Runkel (ed.), *Campaign for President: The Managers Look at '88*. Dover, Mass.: Auburn House.

Eismeier, Theodore, and Philip Pollock III, 1986. "Strategy and Choice in Congressional Elections: The Role of Political Action Committees." *American Journal of Political Science*, 30, 197–213.

    1988. *Business Money and the Rise of Corporate PACs in American Elections*. New York: Quorum Books.

Evans, Diana, 1988. "Oil PACs and Aggressive Contribution Strategies." *Journal of Politics*, 50, 1047–56.

Federal Election Commission, 1977. *FEC Reports on Financial Activity 1975–1976*. Washington, D.C.

    1981. *FEC Reports on Financial Activity 1979–1980*. Washington, D.C.

    1985. *FEC Reports on Financial Activity 1983–1984*. Washington, D.C.

1989. *FEC Reports on Financial Activity 1987–1988.* Washington, D.C.

1993. *FEC Reports on Financial Activity 1991–1992.* Washington, D.C.

Fenno, Richard F., 1973. *Congressmen in Committees.* Boston: Little, Brown.

1978. *Home Style: House Members in Their Districts.* Boston: Little, Brown.

Foley, John, Dennis Britton, and Eugene Everett, Jr., 1980. *Nominating a President: The Process and the Press.* New York: Praeger.

Freeman, Jo, 1986. "The Political Culture of the Democratic and Republican Parties." *Political Science Quarterly,* 101, 327–56.

Geer, John, 1989. *Nominating Presidents.* New York: Greenwood.

Germond, Jack W., and Jules Witcover, 1981. *Blue Smoke and Mirrors.* New York: Viking Press.

1989. *Whose Broad Stripes and Bright Stars? The Trivial Pursuit of the Presidency, 1988.* New York: Warner.

Gerth, Jeff, 1987. "Top Insurance Officials Underwrite Dole Effort." *New York Times,* December 24, B6.

Godwin, R. Kenneth, 1988. *One Billion Dollars of Influence.* Chatham, N.J.: Chatham House.

Godwin, R. Kenneth, and R. C. Mitchell, 1984. "The Impact of Direct Mail on Political Organizations." *Social Science Quarterly,* 65, 829–39.

Goldwin, Robert A., ed., 1980. *Political Parties in the Eighties.* Washington, D.C.: American Enterprise Institute for Public Policy Research.

Gopoian, J. David, "Issue Preference and Candidate Choice in Presidential Primaries." *American Journal of Political Science,* 26, 523–46.

1984. "What Makes PACs Tick: An Analysis of the Allocation Patterns of Economic Interest Groups." *American Journal of Political Science,* 28, 259–77.

Grassmuck, George, 1985. *Before Nomination.* Washington, D.C.: American Enterprise Institute for Public Policy Research.

Green, Donald, and Jonathan Krasno, 1988. "Salvation for the Spendthrift Incumbent: Reestimating the Effects of Campaign Spending in House Elections." *American Journal of Political Science,* 32, 884–907.

1990. "Rebuttal to Jacobson's 'New Evidence for Old Arguments.'" *American Journal of Political Science,* 34, 363–72.

Green, John, 1989. "A Look at the 'Invisible Army': Pat Robertson's Campaign Contributors." Paper given at the annual meeting of the Association for the Advancement of Science, San Francisco.

Green, John, and James Guth, 1984. "Who Is Right and Who Is Left? Varieties of Ideology among Political Contributors." Paper given at the annual meeting of the American Political Science Association, Washington, D.C.

1986. "Big Bucks and Petty Cash: Party and Interest Group Activists in American Politics." In A. Cigler and B. Loomis (eds.), *Interest Group Politics,* 2d edition. Washington, D.C.: CQ Press.

1988a. "The Christian Right in the Republican Party: The Case of Pat Robertson's Contributors." *Journal of Politics,* 50, 150–65.

1988b. "The Price of Power: Republican Party Factionalism in the Reagan Era." Paper given at the annual meeting of the American Political Science Association, Chicago.

Greenfield, Jeff, 1982. *The Real Campaign: How the Media Missed the Story of the 1980 Campaign.* New York: Summit Books.

Gurian, Paul-Henri, 1986. "Resource Allocation Strategies in Presidential Nomination Campaigns." *American Journal of Political Science*, 30, 802–21.

Guth, James, and John Green, 1986. "Faith and Politics: Religion and Ideology among Political Contributors." *American Politics Quarterly*, 14, 186–200.

1987. "The Moralizing Minority: Christian Right Support among Political Activists." *Social Science Quarterly*, 67, 598–610.

1990. "Politics in a New Key: Religiosity and Participation among Political Activists." *Western Political Quarterly*, 43, 153–79.

1991. "God and the GOP: Varieties of Religiosity among Political Contributors." In T. Jelen (ed.), *Religion and American Political Behavior.* New York: Praeger.

Handler, Edward, and John Mulkern, 1982. *Business in Politics: Campaign Strategies of Corporate Political Action Committees.* Lexington, Mass.: Lexington Books.

Harwood, Richard, ed., 1980. *The Pursuit of the Presidency 1980.* New York: Berkeley Books.

Heard, Alexander, 1962. *The Costs of Democracy.* Garden City, N.Y.: Doubleday.

Heard, Alexander, and Michael Nelson, eds., 1987. *Presidential Selection.* Durham, N.C.: Duke University Press.

Hedges, Roman, 1984. "Reasons for Political Involvement: A Study of Contributors to the 1972 Presidential Campaign." *Western Political Quarterly*, 37, 257–71.

Hermson, Paul, 1988. *Party Campaigning in the 1980s.* Cambridge, Mass: Harvard University Press.

1989. "National Party Decisionmaking, Strategies, and Resource Distribution in Congressional Elections." *Western Political Quarterly*, 42, 301–24.

1992. "Campaign Profesionalism and Fundraising in Congressional Elections." *Journal of Politics*, 54, 859–70.

Hertzke, Allen D., 1993. *Echoes of Discontent.* Washington, D.C.: CQ Press.

Jackson, Brooks, 1988. *Honest Graft.* Washington, D.C.: Farragut Publishing Company.

Jackson, John S., III., Jesse C. Brown, and Barbara L. Brown, 1978. "Recruitment, Representation, and Political Values: The 1976 Democratic National Convention Delegates." *American Politics Quarterly*, 6, 187–212.

Jacobson, Gary, 1980. *Money in Congressional Elections.* New Haven: Yale University Press.

1986. "Party Organization and Campaign Resources: Republicans and Democrats in 1982." *Political Science Quarterly*, 100, 603–25.

1990. "The Effects of Campaign Spending in House Elections: New Evidence for Old Arguments." *American Journal of Political Science* 34, 334–62.

Jacobson, Gary, and Samuel Kernell, 1981. *Strategy and Choice in Congressional Elections.* New Haven: Yale University Press.

Jones, Ruth, 1990. "Contributing as Participation." In M. Nugent and J. Johannes (eds.), *Money, Elections, and Democracy.* Boulder, Colo.: Westview.

Jones, Ruth, and Warren Miller, 1985. "Financing Campaigns: Macro Level Innovation and Micro Level Response." *Western Political Quarterly*, 38, 187–210.

Keeter, Scott, and Cliff Zukin, 1983. *Uninformed Choice: The Failure of the New Presidential Nominating System*. New York: Praeger.

Kessel, John, 1980. *Presidential Campaign Politics: Coalition Strategies and Citizen Responses*. Homewood, Ill.: Dorsey.

Kingdon, John W., 1981. *Congressmen's Voting Decisions*. New York: Harper & Row.

Kirkpatrick, Jeane, 1976. *The New Presidential Elite: Men and Women in National Politics*. New York: Russel Sage Foundation.

Latus, Margaret, 1984. "Assessing Ideological PACs: From Outrage to Understanding." In M. Malbin (ed.), *Money and Politics in the United States*. Chatham, N.J.: Chatham House.

Lengle, James, 1981. *Representation and Presidential Primaries: The Democratic Party in the Post-Reform Era*. Westport, Conn.: Greenwood Press.

Levick-Segnatelli, Barbara, 1994. "The Washington Political Action Committee: One Man Can Make a Difference." In R. Biersack, P. Herrnson, and C. Wilcox (eds.), *Risky Business: PAC Decisionmaking in Congressional Elections*. Armonk, N.Y.: M.E. Sharpe.

Magleby, David, and Candice Nelson, 1990. *The Money Chase*. Washington, D.C.: Brookings.

Malbin, Michael, 1984. *Money and Politics in the United States*. Chatham, N.J.: Chatham House.

    1985. "You Get What You Pay for, but Is That What You Want?" In George Grassmuck (ed.), *Before Nomination*. Washington, D.C.: American Enterprise Institute for Public Policy Research.

Marshall, Thomas R., 1981. *Presidential Nominations in a Reform Age*. New York: Praeger.

May, Clifford D., 1987. "A Democrat Whose Forte Is Funds." *New York Times*, April 24, A14.

Miller, Warren, 1988. *Without Consent: Mass-Elite Linkages in American Politics*. Lexington: University of Kentucky Press.

Miller, Warren E., and M. Kent Jennings, 1986. *Parties in Transition: A Longitudinal Study of Party Elites and Party Supporters*. New York: Russell Sage Foundation.

Moore, Jonathan, ed., 1981. *The Campaign for President: 1980 in Retrospect*. Cambridge, Mass.: Ballinger.

    1986. *The Campaign for President: The Managers Look at '84*. Dover, Mass.: Auburn House.

Morin, Richard, 1988. "Giving Twice – To Candidates and their PACs." *Washington Post*, February 7, 17.

Morrison, Donald, ed., 1988. *The Winning of the White House 1988*. New York: *Time*.

Mutch, Robert E., 1988. *Campaigns, Congress, and Courts: The Making of Federal Campaign Finance Law*. New York: Praeger.

Nelson, Candice, 1994. "Women's PACs in the Year of the Woman." In Elizabeth Adell Cook, Sue Thomas, and Clyde Wilcox (eds.), *The Year of the Woman: Myths and Realities*. Boulder, Colo.: Westview.

Nelson, Michael, ed., 1985. *The Elections of 1984*. Washington, D.C.: CQ Press.

1989. *The Elections of 1988.* Washington, D.C.: CQ Press.

Nichols, David, 1988. *Financing Elections.* Glenview, Ill.: Scott, Foresman.

Norrander, Barbara, 1989. "Ideological Representativeness of Presidential Primary Voters." *American Journal of Political Science,* 33, 570–87.

Orren, Gary R., 1985. "The Nomination Process: The Vicissitudes of Candidate Selection." In Michael Nelson (ed.), *The Elections of 1984.* Washington, D.C.: CQ Press.

Overacker, Louise, 1946. *Presidential Campaign Funds.* Boston: Boston University Press.

1974. *Money in Elections.* New York: Arno Press.

Paolino, Philip, 1994. *Candidate Name Recognition and the Dynamics of the Presidential Nomination Process.* Unpublished doctoral dissertation, Duke University Press.

Patterson, Thomas E., 1980. *The Mass Media Election: How Americans Choose Their President.* New York: Praeger.

Polsby, Nelson W., 1983. *Consequences of Party Reform.* Oxford: Oxford University Press.

Polsby, Nelson W., and Aaron Wildavsky, 1991. *Presidential Elections: Contemporary Strategies of American Electoral Politics,* 8th edition. New York: Free Press.

Powell, Lynda W., 1989. "Analyzing Misinformation: Perceptions of Congressional Candidates' Ideologies." *American Journal of Political Science,* 33, 272–93.

Powell, Lynda, with Clifford Brown and Roman Hedges, 1981. "Male and Female Differences in Elite Political Participation: An Examination of the Effects of Socioeconomic and Familial Variables." *Western Political Quarterly,* 34, 31–45.

Ranney, Austin, 1977. *Participation in American Presidential Nominations 1976.* Washington, D.C.: American Enterprise Institute for Public Policy Research.

Rapoport, Daniel, 1979. "Campaign Politics–The Telltale Signs of a Regulated Industry." *National Journal,* January 20, 92–95.

Rapoport, Ronald, Alan Abramowitz, and John McGlennon, 1986. *The Life of the Parties.* Lexington: University of Kentucky Press.

Reiter, Howard L., 1985. *Selecting the President: The Nominating Process in Transition.* Philadelphia: University of Pennsylvania Press.

Rimmerman, Craig, 1994. "New Kids on the Block: National Gay and Lesbian Victory Fund and WISH List in the 1992 Congressional Elections." In Robert Biersack, Paul Herrnson, and Clyde Wilcox (eds.), *Risky Business? PAC Decisionmaking in Congressional Elections.* Armonk, N.Y.: M. E. Sharpe.

Robinson, Michael, 1985. "Where's the Beef? Media and Media Elites in 1984." In Ranney, Austin (ed.), *The American Elections of 1984.* Durham, N.C.: Duke University Press.

Runkel, David, 1989. *Campaign for President: The Managers Look at '88.* Dover, Mass: Auburn House.

Sabato, Larry, 1981. *The Rise of Political Consultants: New Ways of Winning Elections.* New York: Basic Books.

1984. *PAC Power: Inside the World of Political Action Committees.* New

York: Norton.

1988. *The Party's Just Begun: Shaping Political Parties for America's Future.* Boston: Little, Brown.

Salisbury, Robert, 1969. "An Exchange Theory of Interest Groups." *Midwest Journal of Political Science*, 13, 1–32.

Shafer, Byron, 1984. *Quiet Revolution: The Struggle for the Democratic Party and the Shaping of Post Reform Politics.* New York: Russell Sage Foundation.

1986. "Republicans and Democrats as Social Types: Or Notes towards an Ethnography of the Political Parties." *Journal of American Studies*, 20, 341–54.

Shields, Mark, 1994. "High–Stakes Presidential Poker." *Washington Post*, February 6.

Sigelman, Lee, 1993. "'If You Prick Us, Do We Not Bleed? If You Tickle Us, Do We Not Laugh?' Jews and Pocketbook Voting." *Journal of Politics*, 53, 977–92.

Simon, Roger, 1990. *Road Show*. New York: Farrar, Straus & Giroux.

Sniderman, Paul M., Richard A. Brody, and Philip E. Tetlock, 1991. *Reasoning and Choice: Explorations in Political Psychology*. New York: Cambridge University Press.

Snyder, Karen, 1991. "Political Contributors: A Hierarchy among Elites." Presented at the annual meeting of the Midwest Political Science Association, Chicago.

Sorauf, Frank, 1984. *What Price PACs?* New York: Twentieth Century Fund.

1988. *Money in American Elections*. Glenview, Ill.: Scott, Foresman.

1992. *Inside Campaign Finance: Myths and Realities*. New Haven: Yale University Press.

Stark, Steven D., 1988. "The Money Men and the Candidates." *New York Times*, April 17, Section 3, 1.

Stencel, Mark, 1992. "'Bundling' Skirts Campaign Gift Curbs." *Washington Post*, April 20, A1.

Sullam, Bruce, 1988. "The Cash Campaign." *New Republic*, March 14, 9.

Taylor, Paul, 1990. *See How They Run*. New York: Knopf.

Thayer, George, 1973. *Who Shakes the Money Tree*. New York: Simon and Schuster.

Verba, Sidney, and Norman Nie, 1972. *Participation in America*. New York: Harper & Row.

Walker, Jack, 1988. "The Primary Game." *Wilson Quarterly*, 12, 64–77.

Walsh, Edward, 1992. "The More Seed Money, the Better the Harvest: At the Bottom of the Heap, Babbitt Struggles to Raise Funds on the Phone." In Stephen J. Wayne and Clyde Wilcox (eds.), *The Quest for National Office*. New York: St. Martin's.

Watson, Richard A., 1988. *The Presidential Contest*, 3d edition. Washington, D.C.: CQ Press.

Wayne, Stephen J., 1992. *The Road to the White House 1992*. New York: St. Martin's.

Werth, Barry, 1988. "The Incredible Rolodex." *New England Monthly*, July, 37.

Wilcox, Clyde, 1987. "Popular Support for the Moral Majority in 1980: A Second Look." *Social Science Quarterly*, 68, 157–67.

1988a. "Political Action Committees and Abortion: A Longitudinal Analysis." *Women & Politics*, 9, 1–20.

1988b. "PACs and Pluralism: Interest Group Formation and Partisanship." *Polity*, 21, 155–66.

1988c. "I Owe It All to Me: Candidates' Investments in Their Own Campaigns."

American Politics Quarterly, 16, 266–79.

1989a. "Organizational Variables and the Contribution Behavior of Large PACs." *Political Behavior*, 11, 157–73.

1989b. "Share the Wealth: Contributions of Congressional Incumbents to the Campaigns of Other Candidates." *American Politics Quarterly*, 17, 386–408.

1991. "Financing the 1988 Prenomination Campaigns." In Emmett Buell, Jr., and Lee Sigelman (eds.), *Nominating a President*. Knoxville: University of Tennessee Press.

1992. *God's Warriors: The Christian Right in 20th Century America*. Baltimore: The Johns Hopkins University Press.

1994. "Coping with Declining Fortunes: AFL-CIO's Committee on Political Education." In Robert Biersack, Paul Herrnson, and Clyde Wilcox (eds.), *Risky Business? PAC Decisionmaking in Congressional Elections*. Armonk, N.Y.: M.E. Sharpe.

Wilcox, Clyde, Clifford Brown, Jr., and Lynda Powell, 1993a. "Republican Voting among Democratic Party Contributors: A Test of Rival Hypotheses." research note, *Polity*, 26, 127–40.

1993b. "Sex and the Political Contributor: The Gender Gap Among Contributors to Presidential Candidates in 1988." *Political Research Quarterly*, 46, 355–76.

Wilcox, Clyde, and Marc Genest, 1991. "Member PACs as Strategic Actors." *Polity*, 23, 85–91.

Wilcox, Clyde, Lee Sigelman, and Elizabeth Adell Cook, 1989. "Some Like It Hot: Individual Differences in Responses to Group Feeling Thermometers." *Public Opinion Quarterly*, 53, 247–57.

Wilson, James Q., 1973. *Political Organizations*. New York: Basic Books.

Witcover, Jules, 1977. *Marathon: The Pursuit of the Presidency, 1972–1976*. New York: New American Library.

Wright, John, 1985. "PACs, Contributions, and Roll Calls: An Organizational Analysis." *American Political Science Review*, 79, 400–14.

Index